Contents

Hi I'm Hannah!..2

Dedication...3

Introduction: A Premise of Praise!..4

Chapter 1: A Seed of Promise!..7

Chapter 2: In His Presence Exercise...12

Chapter 3: The Ultra with No Sound!..17

Chapter 4: Look Up Dear Child...22

Chapter 5: The Mother with The Issue Of Blood!..27

Chapter 6: Teleo - It Is Finished!...32

Chapter 7: The Miscarriage Is Not the Marriage!..37

Chapter 8: The Elephant In The Room...43

Chapter 9: Weeping Endures for A Night, But Joy Cometh in The Morning..................46

Chapter 10: A Father's Silent Funeral Saying Goodbye in the Bathroom.....................49

Chapter 11: Man to Man: Man Down..53

Chapter 12: The Phoenix Who Rises from The Ashes!................................57

Pregnancy Prayer of Protection!...61

Mommy's Special Excerpt for Hannah..64

About the Author..66

A Heartfelt Thank You from LaTasha and Richard.......................................67

Hi I'm Hannah!

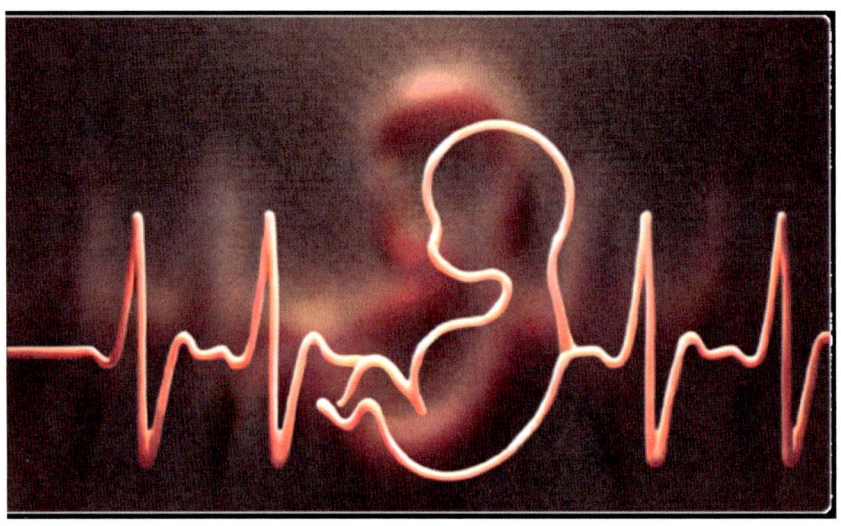

www.hannahsheartbeats.com

www.hannahheartbeats@gmail.com

www.hannahheartbeats@yahoo.com

www.hannahsheartbeats.com

Dedication

This book is dedicated to mothers and fathers across the nation who felt like they were voiceless after losing their child.

God had a divine purpose for your pain, and through these writings, you shall reign!

To my husband who supported me through this journey and listened then yielded to the sweet voice of the Holy Spirit, to help men regain their livelihood and healing—I honor you!

Thank you for your (Rich)ness of spirit and heart to hear it!

For my dear mother Alcee Fullwood Eure, who did not stop praying or believing until her promise of a daughter came into fruition. Because of you, I possess purpose and passion to do his will!

Read it as you rest peacefully in the sweet arms of Jesus! I love you! Thank you!

Jer 29:11
"For I know the plans I have for you," declares the LORD, "plans to prosper you and not to harm you, plans to give you hope and a future".

—LaTasha

Introduction: A Premise of Praise!

Stripped Bare, Yet Seeking Solace

Have you ever felt like everything in your life was stripped away? Did you think that the existence you have lived would be encrusted with trials? Did you find yourself seeking solace in a being that you cannot touch but knew beyond a shadow of a doubt that HE was there? These questions resonate deeply with the human experience, don't they? They echo the cries of a heart laid bare, a soul reaching out through the fog of despair toward a light that promises hope. The God I know is a very present help in a time of need. He is the one who, when everything in life seems barren, can birth forth fruit from the hardest of trials. This truth is not just a platitude—it's a lifeline, a divine reality that has carried me through the darkest valleys of my life. And this book will unravel a life that has endured a significant loss! It will depict a process of the beautiful seed that grew inside my womb—one framed with heartache but catapulted into a new direction. One where, when the author had absolutely nothing to lean on but the indwelling of the Holy Spirit, the divine word of God brought joy, edification, and light through power and His divine connections. Even in loss, He restores!

The Unspoken Pain of Miscarriage

There are moments in life when the world expects us to move on quickly, when certain scenarios are brushed under the rug as though they never happened. But when this happens, it leaves a cold hole in the soul of the one who encountered the pain. Miscarriage is one such scenario—a loss so profound, yet so often minimized by those who haven't walked its lonely road. I want to offer light at the end of that tunnel. You see, this book will discuss various methods on how to overcome trauma and heal from miscarriage. Upon thousands of words that have been encrypted on the pages of Instagram and Facebook, women across the globe move on once they have lost a child. Some of these precious gems have included close friends who have lost multiple babies and were unable to see their seeds come into fruition. Others were blessed with many children after their ordeals. I've watched their journeys, wept with them, and marveled at the resilience God has woven into the fabric of their spirits. Yet I have come to the realization that some beings believe that if your child didn't make it into existence physically, that it wasn't purposeful or that the life of that seed didn't count. I am here to tell every woman who has lost a child that the precious life that was created, no matter how short its existence, was special in the eyes of God.

A Message for Every Heart

For the women and men who have never had anyone to talk to, this book is for you! For the women who have tried for numerous years and experienced the hurt, trauma, and pain of delivering stillborn children, this is for you. To the ladies who have watched their stomachs stretch and grow, then woken up the next day to find it deflating slowly like a balloon, these words are for you. Finally, for those who still do not have a child or have accepted that it is fine to be a "mother to many" for other children in this world, this was written for you. The Bible outlines in Psalm 107:19-20, "Then they cried to the Lord in their trouble, and he saved them from their distress. He sent out his word and healed them; he rescued them from the grave." Declare—I AM HEALED!

God's Refuge in Our Trouble

This scripture, women and men of God, is a swift reminder that God is our refuge. He is a very present help in a time of need. Even when you don't have the words to form out of your bellies due to the hurt—HE carries you through! As the Father sends out His word to heal you, RECEIVE in this moment by taking a moment to reflect and do these basic steps:

Steps to Healing

- **Spend Time in Worship with the Father:** Intimacy is IN-TO-HIM-I-SEE! He sees the brokenness, the embarrassment, the hurt, and the pain. But like the wing of a tender bird, He can heal you and make you whole again!
  Surrender: There is a gospel song that goes, "I surrender all… I surrender all… All to Thee my blessed Savior, I surrender all." The biblical meaning of surrendering all to God is relinquishing your control, plans, and wisdom to Him! It is giving up one's will and trusting in God to provide for your needs.
  Spiritual Principles: Utilizing the principles of forgiveness, love, courage, and patience through the healing process not only brings hope to the trial but helps you decipher and see what God is doing in the moment. "Hope deferred makes the heart sick." This proverb means that when hopes and dreams are delayed or denied, it can lead to feelings of sadness, disappointment, or despair. So, the longer a person goes without seeing their hope realized, the more likely they are to become discouraged. Allow HIM to show you how to forgive yourself. He is imparting the courage and granting you the patience to endure!
- **Participate In Your Healing:** Many years ago, I learned about an acronym called T.A.P., which means "Taking An Active Part!" Taking an active part means acknowledging your pain, talking through each moment, and giving yourself grace through the processes. In Matthew 15:26, the Bible says, "Healing is the children's bread," which means it is part of our inheritance. It means HEALING BELONGS TO GOD'S CHILDREN. It is your right! It is your portion! He cares about every detail that you are going through and wants to set you free from all hurt and pain!
  Receive Your Healing: One thing about the body is that when it holds on to pain, unforgiveness, hurt, bitterness, or unresolved trauma, it manifests in the form of illness. So, it is imperative to take the proper time to heal and embrace it! In the scripture Isaiah 53:4-5, it states, "For he was wounded for my transgressions, he was bruised for my iniquities; the chastisement of his peace is upon thee that by your stripes, (insert your names) are healed." This means that the Father took every sickness known to man and bore it for us! He knew before

we were formed what healing we would need. But doesn't it bring peace to know that He already provided a remedy in advance because He loves us that much!
- **Seek Solace:** In times of uncertainty, finding comfort and strength can be found in scripture. In Isaiah 41:10, it states, "Fear not, for I am with you; be not dismayed, for I am your God; I will strengthen you, I will help you, I will uphold you with my righteous hand." This is a sure foundation that you can seek peace and strength in the midst of the storm. So remember, the peace that the Father gives surpasses our understanding but is a premise to stand in faith.

Petition The Father: In John 14:14, it says, "If you ask ANYTHING in my name, I will do it!" Prayer is simply talking to God. So, He waits patiently for us to cry out, and due to His heart toward us, He delivers! So, ask and ye shall receive, saints. Don't be afraid to step onto the water. He is there to carry you and walk you through every process.

Chapter 1: A Seed of Promise!

A Prayer from Childhood

What is a promise from God? It's a question that has echoed through my soul since I was a little girl, kneeling in prayer, whispering pleas to a God I couldn't see but felt with every fiber of my being. When I was younger, I would always pray and ask the Lord to not let me have a child out of wedlock. I grew up in a fatherless home. Even though I was conceived in marriage, my father, who I reconciled with one year before he died, was never present in my home. His absence left a void, a jagged edge in my heart that shaped how I saw the world. I saw a plethora of brokenness around me, and a lot of it stemmed from fatherless households. As a result, my big brother took on many roles like providing, taking me to dance classes, picking me up from school, daily visits to the babysitter, and protecting me at all costs. He was my shield, my stand-in, my hero. So, I always wanted my child(ren) to have an active husband and father in the home. That desire wasn't just a wish—it was a prayer, a vow I made to God, a seed planted in the soil of my spirit. God heard those prayers and answered them in my adulthood. In Psalms 89:33-34, it states, "But I will not withdraw my steadfast love from him, nor will I make my faithfulness a lie. My covenant I will not violate, nor will I alter the word that has gone out from my lips!" God does not negate on His promises, daughters and sons! This is a declaration He declared to His people! So, no matter what you have gone through in the area of childbearing, know that through His divine sovereignty, He SHALL bring His promises to pass!

The Promise Manifests

The promise of bringing forth a child manifested in the fall of 2018. It was my favorite season because it is a time when seeds are planted in preparation for a harvest. There's something sacred about fall—the crisp air, the golden leaves, the quiet anticipation of life waiting beneath the surface. Business was booming, and students were in constant rehearsals, preparing for competition in the spring. But in the midst of the preparedness, something odd was going on with my body. You see, I would fall asleep, whether it was napping or for the night, and would wake up with these sharp, stabbing pains in my lower abdomen and stomach. Unfortunately, they would only subside if I curled into a fetal position. At first, I brushed it off as fatigue or stress, but after a few weeks, the persistence of the pain gnawed at me. I decided to schedule a doctor appointment to get a full check-up.

A Joyful Discovery

On the day of the visit, we followed all the protocol for check-ins and were finally led to our room to see the doctor. The physician assessed the situation and decided to administer a pregnancy test. I took it quickly, my heart pounding with a mix of curiosity and trepidation, and we waited to receive the results. The doctor came in with this huge smile on her face and announced with boldness, "Congratulations, you are pregnant!" My husband had the biggest smile on his face, and we were both ecstatic. Joy erupted in that sterile room—a joy so pure it felt like a gift straight from heaven. He did proceed to ask why the sharp pains were transpiring, and we were reassured that active and careful monitoring would take place as we embarked on this new journey. We proceeded to get counsel regarding protocol on vitamins, water intake, doctor visits, procedures for my age, and everything needed to help this process be a success! As a result, we left the facility ready to embrace our new walk of faith!

A New Journey Begins

This was my very first pregnancy, and it would be our third child as a family. My husband already had two children from his previous marriage, and their presence in our lives was a blessing—a lively tapestry of love and chaos. But this child was mine, ours, a seed of promise I'd carried in my heart since girlhood. As we prepared for our new addition, things began to take a sudden turn and would bring an unexpected journey that only faith, hope, and love would bring us through!

Facing Uncertainty

That Sunday, I started bleeding. The sight of red sent a jolt of fear through me, a silent scream that something was wrong. So, we went to Urgent Care. In the office, they performed an ultrasound. We were told the baby was fine, but my numbers were not increasing, which was a red flag for the baby and its growth! The HCG (human chorionic gonadotropin) levels were not doubling as they expected, which ended up with the doctor requesting weekly visits to monitor the baby. At the time of the visit, they were able to measure the growth of the baby and announce the number of weeks that I had been carrying. So, I followed the care instructions that were given, scheduled the next appointment, and continued using cautionary measures to ensure this would be a smooth process.

A Glimpse of Life

On my next visit, a week later, they took blood and performed other pertinent tests. My little tummy was growing quickly. To see a seed evolve was not only beautiful but a gentle reminder that God gives life, and that life more abundantly! At that moment, two things were going on. I had not stopped bleeding, and the numbers were still not increasing. However, this visit was extra special because they did an ultrasound. It took a while for them to locate the baby, who was hiding very low in my womb. But a miracle happened. It was at the very moment when I heard a "thump, thump, thump," I left that visit with a printout of the baby's heartbeat. I could see their tiny little image, and it was a day I will never forget, one I will hold tight in the crevices of my spirit!

Hope Amidst the Storm

When God implants a seed in your womb and fulfills a lifelong promise, it does something to your faith. It produces hope! Hope, by definition, is "a feeling of expectation and desire for a certain thing to happen; a feeling of trust." So, you must put your trust in the Father to see you through! On the positive end, we had just seen the baby's vibrant heartbeat. On the other, they were concerned about the progress of my numbers. In the moments when I would hear the adverse news, it was then that the word of God had to become evident in our life. In Deuteronomy 31:6, it states, "Be strong and courageous. Do not fear or be in dread of them, for it is the Lord your God who goes with you. He will not leave you or forsake you." So, in this process, we were never alone! He was providing the strength to face this challenge with faith that was rooted and grounded in Him and His word. Courage, my friends, stems from knowing God's constant presence and realizing that He is readily available!

A Sacred Echo
That heartbeat—thump, thump, thump—was a symphony of life, a melody of promise that drowned out the fear, if only for a moment. I held that ultrasound printout like a treasure, tracing the blurry outline of my baby with my fingers. It was tangible proof that God had heard my prayers, that He had woven this little life into existence. Genesis 1:27 reminds us, "So God created mankind in his own image, in the image of God he created them." Even in those early weeks, my child bore His image, a reflection of divine love nestled within me. For my husband, this was a third child, a new thread in the fabric of his fatherhood. For me, it was a first—a sacred initiation into motherhood that I'd dreamed of since I was a girl watching my brother fill the gaps my father left behind.

Trusting God's Faithfulness
The promise I'd clung to wasn't just about avoiding the pain I'd seen growing up; it was about trusting God to build something whole, something beautiful. In Isaiah 55:11, God declares, "So is my word that goes out from my mouth: It will not return to me empty, but will accomplish what I desire and achieve the purpose for which I sent it." My prayer as a young girl wasn't a fleeting wish—it was a word spoken into the heart of a God who keeps His promises. And in the fall of 2018, that word bore fruit. The season itself felt like a metaphor—seeds planted in hidden places, waiting to burst forth. I saw my pregnancy as a harvest of faith, a testament to God's faithfulness across the years.

A Test of Faith
But the sharp pains were a whisper of trouble, a shadow creeping into the light of our joy. Curling into a fetal position to ease the ache felt symbolic—like I was cradling the life within me, willing it to stay. When the doctor confirmed the pregnancy, I exhaled a breath I didn't know I'd been holding. My husband's smile mirrored mine, and in that moment, we were united in hope. The counsel we received—vitamins, hydration, regular check-ups—was a roadmap we followed diligently, believing it would lead us to a healthy baby. Leaving that office, I felt like a pioneer stepping into uncharted territory, armed with faith and love.

Anchored Through the Storm
Yet faith doesn't shield us from storms—it anchors us through them. That Sunday, when the bleeding began, fear clawed at my chest. The drive to Urgent Care was a blur, my prayers a jumbled stream of "Please, God, let them be okay." The ultrasound screen flickered to life, and there was our baby—small, but real. The reassurance that the baby was fine was a lifeline, but the stagnant HCG levels were a warning bell I couldn't unhear. Numbers became my enemy, a clinical measure of a miracle I wanted to protect with my whole being. Weekly visits stretched before us, a rhythm of hope and dread intertwined.

Abundant Life Unfolding
The next visit brought a bittersweet gift. My tummy, rounding with life, was a quiet marvel. John 10:10 echoed in my mind: "I have come that they may have life, and have it to the fullest." This was abundant life unfolding within me, a seed sprouting despite the odds. The ultrasound wand pressed against my skin, searching, until that glorious sound filled the room—thump, thump, thump. My baby's heartbeat was a declaration of existence, a pulse of promise I could hold onto. The printout I clutched as we left was more than paper—it was a relic of a moment when hope outshone fear.

Courage in Uncertainty
But hope is a fragile thing, easily bruised by uncertainty. The bleeding persisted, the numbers refused to climb, and I found myself wrestling with a faith that felt both unshakeable and unsteady. My husband, steady and strong, stood beside me, his own grief tempered by the children he already held. For me, this scare loomed larger, a first dream teetering on the edge. Yet God's word cut through the noise. In Joshua 1:9, He commands, "Have I not commanded you? Be strong and courageous. Do not be afraid; do not be discouraged, for the Lord your God will be with you wherever you go." Courage wasn't the absence of fear—it was the choice to trust God's presence in the midst of it.

A Life Written by God
That heartbeat lingered in my memory, a sacred echo of a life that was mine. Psalm 139:13-16 became my refuge: "For you created my inmost being; you knit me together in my mother's womb… Your eyes saw my unformed body; all the days ordained for me were written in your book before one of them came to be." My baby's days were few, but they were written by God, purposeful and precious. This truth didn't erase the pain—it gave it meaning. And in that meaning, I found the strength to keep walking, to keep hoping, to keep trusting.

Devotional Call to Action: Standing on His Promises
Scripture Reflection: "Be strong and courageous. Do not fear or be in dread of them, for it is the Lord your God who goes with you. He will not leave you or forsake you" (Deuteronomy 31:6, NIV).
Meditation: Close your eyes and imagine God planting a seed of promise in your heart. Maybe it was a dream you held, or a hope you still carry. Hear His voice whispering, "I am with you." Your fear of loss doesn't negate His promise—it refines it. Sit with that truth, letting it anchor your soul.
Prayer: Lord, You are the keeper of promises, the giver of life. I bring my fears, my pain, and my unanswered questions to You. Thank You for the seed You planted in me, for the heartbeat I hear, and the love I feel. Strengthen me with Your courage, hold me with Your presence, and renew my hope in Your unfailing word. In Jesus' name, Amen.

Action Steps:

- **Worship:** Sing or listen to "Promises" by Maverick City Music, letting the lyrics remind you of God's faithfulness.
- **Reflect:** Write down a promise God has fulfilled in your life, no matter how small. Then write one you're still waiting on, trusting Him with the outcome.
- **Pray:** Speak Deuteronomy 31:6 over yourself daily this week, claiming God's presence in your journey.
- **Rest:** Take a quiet moment to hold something symbolic of your baby—a photo, a keepsake, or even your own hands—and release them to God's care.
Encouragement: Your seed of promise matters. Whether it is growing to fruition or being nourished by God, it is seen, known, and loved. Stand strong—He's carrying you through every step.

Chapter 2: In His Presence Exercise

A Fragile Dance

The days after hearing my baby's heartbeat were a fragile dance between hope and uncertainty. The bleeding hadn't stopped, the numbers still lagged, and each doctor's visit felt like a tightrope walk over a chasm of fear. My husband and I clung to the promise we'd been given, but the weight of what might come pressed heavily on my spirit. It was in those moments—when the silence of the night amplified my worries—that I learned to seek God's presence in a way I never had before. I want to share with you an exercise that became my lifeline, a way to step into His peace amid the storm. It's simple, yet profound, and it begins with this invitation: Please take a moment and visualize the presence of God.

Step I: Close Your Eyes
It started with closing my eyes—not just to block out the world, but to turn inward, to shut the door on the chaos of medical updates and unanswered questions. In the darkness behind my eyelids, I could begin to sense Him, the One who promised in Psalm 46:1, "God is our refuge and strength, an ever-present help in trouble." Closing my eyes was an act of trust, a surrender to a God I couldn't see with my physical sight but knew was near. For me, it was a way to quiet the noise—the beeping machines, the doctor's cautious tone, the hum of the car on the way home. I invite you to do the same now. Close your eyes, dear one, and let the world fade. Let it be just you and Him.

Step II: Position Yourself in a Posture of Prayer
Next, I'd position myself in a posture of prayer. Sometimes it was kneeling by my bed, forehead pressed to the cool sheets, tears soaking the fabric. Other times, it was sitting in a chair, hands open on my lap, as if offering my fears to Him. There's something powerful about aligning your body with your soul's cry. James 4:8 says, "Come near to God and he will come near to you." That physical posture became a bridge, a way to draw close when my heart felt miles away. Whether you kneel, sit, or stand, position yourself now in a way that says, "I'm here, Lord. I need You." Let your body echo your longing for His presence.

Step III: Invite Him In! INTIMACY—In-To-Him-I-See! Open Your Heart!
Then, I'd invite Him in. INTIMACY—In-To-Him-I-See! It's a phrase I coined to remind myself that true closeness with God means letting Him see me—really see me. I opened my heart, raw and trembling, and said, "Come, Lord. Enter this pain, this fear, this hope." After that ultrasound, when I saw my baby's tiny form, I wanted God to see the love I carried for that little life. I wanted Him to see the dread that crept in with every spot of blood. Revelation 3:20 promises, "Here I am! I stand at the door and knock. If anyone hears my voice and opens the door, I will come in." So, invite Him now. Open your heart wide—let Him see the hurt you carry, the questions you can't voice. He's waiting to step in.

Step IV: Offer Gratitude and Praise!
Even in the uncertainty, I learned to offer gratitude and praise. I'd thank Him for the day—for the breath in my lungs, for my husband's steady hand in mine, for the students whose laughter filled my days. I thanked Him for the miracle of that heartbeat he's graced me with. Philippians 4:6 urges, "Do not be anxious about anything, but in every situation, by prayer and petition, with thanksgiving, present your requests to God." Gratitude shifted my focus from what I might lose to what I still had—His love, His presence, His promises. Take a moment now to thank Him. Praise Him for the day, for the small graces in your life, for the child he's graced you with. Let praise rise like incense before Him.

Step V: If Anything Rises to the Surface, Let Him Deal with Them!
As I sat in His presence, things would rise to the surface—worries about the baby, cares of this life, grace toward myself for not being "strong enough," family issues from my fatherless past, previous hurts, finances strained by medical bills, car troubles, our marriage in the midst of this trial. I'd name them, one by one, and hand them over. 1 Peter 5:7 says, "Cast all your anxiety on him because he cares for you." I saw Him take each burden—the fear of miscarriage, the guilt that whispered I'd failed—and I let Him deal with them. What's rising for you now? Worries, hurts, thoughts of losing your child? Name them, see them in your mind, and release them into His hands. He's big enough to carry them all.

Step VI: See Him in Front of You
I began to see Him in front of me—in the waiting room with its sterile chairs, the doctor's office with its cold instruments, the ride home with my husband's quiet strength beside me. I pictured Jesus there, His eyes full of compassion, His hand on my shoulder. Isaiah 43:2 became real: "When you pass through the waters, I will be with you; and when you pass through the rivers, they will not sweep over you." He was with me when the technician searched for that heartbeat, when the doctor's face tightened with concern, when we drove home in silence. See Him now in your story—wherever your cares unfolded. Picture Him in the hospital, at home, in the quiet moments after. He was there, and He is here.

Step VII: Talk to Him Openly Without Fear! Surrender!
With Him before me, I'd talk to Him openly, without fear. Prayer is simply talking with God, and I poured out my heart—no filter, no pretense. "Lord, I'm scared. I want this baby so much. I don't know how to let go if I have to." I surrendered my plans, my control, my strength. Matthew 11:28-29 invites, "Come to me, all you who are weary and burdened, and I will give you rest… For my yoke is easy and my burden is light." Surrender wasn't weakness—it was rest. Talk to Him now. Tell Him about your fears and losing the baby, your pain, your hopes. Surrender it all—let His rest wash over you like a gentle tide.

Step VIII: Share Your Thoughts, Embracing Challenges in His Strength
I'd share my thoughts—how I planned to take each day by faith, to face the bleeding and the numbers and the waiting, not in my own power, but in His. I'd say, "God, I don't

know what's next, but I'll trust You. Give me Your strength." 2 Corinthians 12:9 reassured me, "My grace is sufficient for you, for my power is made perfect in weakness." My weakness—my fear, my grief—was where His strength shone brightest. Share your thoughts with Him now. How will you face tomorrow's challenges—your baby's aftermath—in His strength, not yours? Speak it out, let faith rise.

Step IX: Write It Down in Your Journal
Finally, I'd write it down in my journal—an act of faith to record what He spoke to me. "Hold on, daughter. I see your baby. I see you." I'd note scriptures like Psalm 139:16: "All the days ordained for me were written in your book before one of them came to be." That little life, so valuable, was etched in His story. Writing anchored me, a tangible step to heed His instructions. Grab your journal now. Write what you felt, what He said, any scriptures that stirred your heart. Let it be a testament to your time in His presence.

Expanding the Narrative: A Journey to His Presence
This exercise wasn't just a list—it was my survival. After that second ultrasound, when the heartbeat thumped through the room, I went home and sat with God. I closed my eyes, positioned myself in prayer, and invited Him into the tangle of joy and dread. I thanked Him for my husband, for my bonus children who called me Tasha, for the promise fulfilled in that tiny life. But the worries came—would this baby make it? Could my body sustain them? I saw Him in the doctor's office, His presence a steady hand as the technician frowned at the screen. I talked to Him, surrendered my need to fix it, and leaned into His strength. In my journal, I wrote, "Lord, You are enough," and Psalm 23:4 came to mind: "Even though I walk through the valley of the shadow of death, I will fear no evil, for you are with me."

Bridging Our Experiences
For my husband, this experience was different—he had his two children, a foundation I didn't yet have. My grief was a first, a raw wound where motherhood was etching a new beginning. But in His presence, I found a bridge between our pains. God met me there, whispering worth into my emptiness. Hebrews 4:16 says, "Let us then approach God's throne of grace with confidence, so that we may receive mercy and find grace to help us in our time of need." That grace held me when the bleeding worsened, when the numbers whispered loss, when I faced what was coming.

Clinging to Him in the Waiting
This chapter isn't about the end of the story—it's about the middle, the waiting, the clinging to Him. Maybe you're there too—for peace amidst the storm. This exercise can be your lifeline, as it was mine. It's not about erasing the pain; it's about finding Him in it. Romans 8:38-39 promises, "Neither death nor life... nor anything else in all creation, will be able to separate us from the love of God that is in Christ Jesus our Lord." Your circumstance can't separate you—He's holding you close.

Devotional Call to Action: Resting in His Presence
Scripture Reflection: "Come to me, all you who are weary and burdened, and I will give you rest" (Matthew 11:28, NIV).
Meditation: Picture yourself in God's presence right now. See Him sitting with you, His eyes full of love, His arms open. Your qualms of a possible miscarriage—whether early or late—left a mark, but it didn't leave you alone. Rest in the truth that He carries your burden with you.
Prayer: Father, I come to You weary from the possibility of loss. I invite You into this pain, thanking You for Your presence that never leaves. Take my worries, my grief, my questions, and give me Your rest. Help me walk each day in Your strength, trusting You with my healing. In Jesus' name, Amen.

Action Steps:

- **Practice:** Spend 5-10 minutes doing the "In His Presence Exercise" above, step by step.
- **Journal:** Write what surfaced—your fears and losing the baby—and a promise from God that spoke to you (e.g., Psalm 46:1, Matthew 11:28).
- **Share:** Tell a trusted friend one thing God showed you in His presence today.
- **Rest:** Light a candle and sit quietly with God, letting His peace settle over you.
Encouragement: The thought of loss is heavy, but His presence is heavier still—strong enough to hold you, gentle enough to heal you. Step into it today; He's waiting.

Chapter 3: The Ultra with No Sound!

A Shift in the Air

Another week went by, and it was time for our next visit. The rhythm of these appointments had become a lifeline—each one a chance to hear that heartbeat again, to see our baby thriving despite the bleeding and the stagnant numbers. But that day felt different from the start. The interesting portion about this day was when I left work. As I entered my truck, there was an odd feeling in my spirit. It wasn't just a passing unease—it was a heaviness, a quiet whisper that something was shifting. I stood in the parking lot with tears running down my cheeks. But I wasn't sure if it was the emotions of being pregnant, the red flags that kept being presented each week from the nurses, the toxic teaching environment I was in daily, or just fear of the unknown. Looking back, I know now it was my spirit letting me know that what was about to transpire would be a day that changed the course of our trajectory, where we could only hold on to God's unchanging hand!

A Shared Hope

My husband ventured to this appointment with me, excited about the new journey we were embracing as a unit. His optimism was a steady light, a contrast to the shadows gathering in my heart. He'd been a father twice before, and this third child—my first—bound us in a shared hope. The wait was over an hour, each tick of the clock stretching my nerves thinner. They finally called us in. I went to the bathroom first due to the time that had passed, a mundane detail that grounded me in the moment. So, we get into our designated room, the ultrasound machine is hooked up to me, and then this dead silence hits the room. It wasn't the silence of anticipation I'd felt before—it was a void, a stillness that swallowed the thump, thump, thump I'd clung to. The doctor's voice cut through it: "I'm sorry, your ultrasound is covered in blood (the black on the screen). You lost the baby!" I immediately started bawling inconsolably. The words crashed over me like a tidal wave, pulling me under. My husband, with his sweet heart, paused to comfort me and hold me in his arms. He was so optimistic. So that night, we were scheduled to see a Lakers game. He was in disbelief but held faith at the same time. His response was, "Can we come back next week to be sure? Maybe it's a mistake in the machine?" She began to give me options on how to pass the baby. There was no waiting—she just got right to the point.

Facing the Options

We were told about a D&C, which stands for "dilation and curettage," a minor surgical procedure to remove tissue from the uterus. The next option was to pass the baby through medication. She informed me it would feel like actual labor pains. I had never been pregnant, and the news came so fast, I just chose the second option. But to respect my husband's wishes, we chose to complete one more ultrasound that following Friday, to ensure what she saw was accurate. He wanted me to enjoy that night. We left that doctor with an array of emotions. My husband was staying optimistic. I, on the other hand, didn't know what to really feel or say, to be honest. But I knew we were not alone and that God was by our side one hundred percent of the way. The Bible says in

Hebrews 13:5, "I will never leave you nor forsake you!" It's a promise from God that He will always support and be with His people. That word "leave" in the Greek is "enkataleipo," which conveys the idea of "to be left behind" or, in English terms, "to be abandoned." Now, isn't that profound? The Father will never abandon us or desist from being by our side. That is a stability that the world could never offer!

Finding Joy Amidst Sorrow
The game was amazing. Even though our hearts were heavy, it was great to see happy victories taking place amidst our news. The roar of the crowd, the flash of purple and gold—it was a temporary escape, a glimpse of joy in a day marked by sorrow. We went to dinner with close friends afterwards. I started crying at the table. My friend asked, "What's wrong?" I could hear her clearly, but my lips wouldn't form any words. The grief had stolen my voice, leaving me mute in a sea of chatter. I was grateful to break bread because it is through times of eating that your mind, body, and spirit are restored. Even though it was only a few hours, it was a pleasure to see good in the midst of heartache and pain. I want to encourage you that when you lose a child, never stay alone during the beginning, middle, or end processes. Find people who can be by your side—who will listen and not judge, a mom who has experienced loss herself. The Bible says in Hebrews 4:15 that "He was touched by the feelings of our infirmities." This means the Lord empathizes with our challenges and is able to provide help. But having a friend who also endured the trial can also comfort and support because God the Father has already carried them through the processes and given them the divine wisdom to help walk you through!

Expanding the Narrative: Clinging to His Unchanging Hand
That day in the parking lot, as tears streaked my face, I didn't yet know the full weight of what awaited me. The toxic environment at work—colleagues who drained rather than uplifted—had already worn me thin. The red flags from the nurses, week after week, had planted seeds of doubt I tried to uproot with faith. And the pregnancy itself—my first—had stirred a whirlwind of emotions: joy, fear, wonder, exhaustion. Standing there, I felt a premonition, a nudge from the Holy Spirit that this wasn't just hormones or fatigue. It was a warning, a preparation for a seismic shift. Psalm 62:5-6 became my whisper: "Yes, my soul, find rest in God; my hope comes from him. Truly he is my rock and my salvation; he is my fortress, I will not be shaken." I didn't feel unshaken then, but I held onto the promise that He was.

The Silence That Shattered
In the ultrasound room, that silence was a dagger. I'd grown to love the sound of life, that thump, thump, thump that tethered me to my baby. Its absence was a void I couldn't comprehend. When the doctor spoke, her words were clinical, final—"You lost the baby." I shattered. My sobs were a primal cry, a mother's wail for a child she'd never hold. My husband's arms around me were a lifeline, his optimism a buoy in my storm. He couldn't believe it—not yet. "Can we come back next week?" he asked, grasping for hope, for a glitch in the machine. I wanted to believe him, to cling to that possibility, but the black on the screen haunted me. Blood where life should have been. The doctor's options—D&C or medication—rushed at me like a freight train. I chose medication, too

dazed to process, too new to pregnancy to know what "labor pains" would mean for a loss. We agreed to one more ultrasound, a compromise for his faith and my fragility.

God's Unfailing Presence
Leaving that office, I was a mosaic of emotions—grief, numbness, disbelief. My husband's positivity was a gift, a reflection of his trust in God's goodness even when I couldn't see it. For him, this was a third child lost, a sorrow layered atop the life he'd built with his other two. For me, it was a first—a dream snuffed out before it could breathe. Yet Hebrews 13:5 anchored us: "I will never leave you nor forsake you." That Greek word "enkataleipo" struck deep—God wouldn't abandon me, wouldn't leave me behind in this pain. In a world that shifts and breaks, His presence was my rock. Deuteronomy 32:4 echoed, "He is the Rock, his works are perfect, and all his ways are just." Even this loss, unjust as it felt, was held in His perfect hands.

Restoration in Community
The Lakers game was a surreal reprieve. The crowd's cheers, the players' triumphs—it was a slice of normalcy, a reminder that life persisted even as mine crumbled. Dinner with friends was harder. The tears came unbidden, spilling over my plate. My friend's gentle "What's wrong?" pierced the fog, but I couldn't speak. The loss was too fresh, too raw. Breaking bread with them, though, was a quiet restoration—a nod to Ecclesiastes 4:9-10: "Two are better than one… If either of them falls down, one can help the other up." I didn't eat alone that night, and I didn't grieve alone either. My friend, who'd lost a child herself, didn't press me to talk. She just sat with me, her presence a silent sermon of survival.

A Lesson in Connection
That night taught me something vital: isolation is the enemy of healing. When miscarriage strikes, the beginning is shock, the middle is sorrow, the end is acceptance—but none should be faced alone. Hebrews 4:15 says Jesus was "touched by the feelings of our infirmities." He felt my anguish, my husband's quiet hope, and He met us there. But God also sent earthly comforters—friends, family, those who'd walked this road. 2 Corinthians 1:4 promises, "He comforts us in all our troubles, so that we can comfort those in any trouble with the comfort we ourselves receive from God." My friend's presence at that table was God's comfort made flesh, a lifeline I urge you to seek too.

Devotional Call to Action: Held by His Unchanging Hand
Scripture Reflection: "I will never leave you nor forsake you" (Hebrews 13:5, NIV).
Meditation: Picture God's hand holding yours—steady, warm, unchanging. Your miscarriage didn't push Him away; it drew Him closer. See Him in that moment of loss—the silent ultrasound, the tears, the questions—and know He never left. Let His presence be your peace.
Prayer: Lord, You are my Rock when everything shakes. I felt abandoned by my loss, but You promise never to leave. Hold me now—my broken heart, my empty womb, my silent grief. Comfort me with Your presence and guide me to others who can share this

load. Thank You for staying. In Jesus' name, Amen.

Action Steps:

- **Reach Out:** Call or text a friend who understands loss. Share one feeling from your miscarriage and let them listen.
- **Reflect:** Write in your journal about a moment you felt God's presence in your grief, pairing it with Hebrews 13:5.
- **Worship:** Sing or listen to "Great Is Thy Faithfulness," letting the words remind you of His unchanging nature.
- **Rest:** Sit with a cup of tea or a warm blanket, imagining God's arms around you, and breathe in His peace.
  Encouragement: You're not abandoned—never were, never will be. Your baby's silence didn't silence God's love. Lean into Him and those He sends; you're held through every tear.

Chapter 4: Look Up Dear Child

A Week of Dread

- The next week was one we both dreaded. The time had come to pass our child, our precious seed who was growing so delicately in my stomach. I would rub my stomach to soothe the baby, read Bible verses, and pray with authority daily so our child would understand the power it carried in Christ. I'd whisper Psalm 139:14 over my womb: "I praise you because I am fearfully and wonderfully made; your works are wonderful, I know that full well." She was our precious unfolding in route to the bathroom, a testament to answered prayers.

, a testament to answered prayers. We went to the doctor. A final confirmation was given through an ultrasound to let us know for sure that the baby had miscarried. Some may wonder why I waited another week. But this seed of promise was also my husband's. So it was extremely important to honor his wishes and give him that final dose of hope that his heart so patiently longed for. I was given instructions by the physician on how to take the medication and followed them when I got home. I re-showered to relax and be at peace in the comfort of our own room.

The Pain Begins

As the medicine kicked in, the pain began to increase. I yelled profusely in discomfort. The labor pains were so intense that all I could do was scream. To be honest, this was my very first pregnancy. So I had no idea the magnitude of the pain I was about to endure. Imagine lying in your home, passing your child, with no epidural in sight. You veer to the right and left to see your husband and friend. But you are the one with the assignment to clear the baby from your womb. In addition, I had some type of effect from the medication. So my bowels were running at times while pieces of the baby were being eliminated into the toilet. Seeing the tissue and particles from our baby hurt my soul. It was so tough to see. It was an experience I wouldn't wish on my worst enemy. So, for hours, I would run back and forth from my bed to the bathroom, which luckily was directly in the master bedroom. The pain was severe, but it was awful. If I were a doctor, I would never offer that option to the patient. It was something I felt needed to be administered in a hospital room where you could be monitored thoroughly. I lost track of time. I just remember seeing pieces of the baby, who had literally passed a week before, floating in the toilet. Due to sanitary reasons, it had to be flushed. That was how I said goodbye to our precious seed!

A Broken Night

The night just became a blur. I got up so many times, I lost count. I didn't really have any words to express or convey! It was literally one of the most broken days of my life. If I could offer any words of encouragement to a woman who has to pass a child, it would be to just "look up," because it is in your distress, and in those precious moments, that God will give you the strength needed to carry you all the way through. No man, no friend, no doctor, no partner, no sibling, not even the comfort of a mother could give you the strength to pass a seed from your womb. It was ONLY because of the power and might of the Lord.

A Husband's Memory
In asking my husband what he recalls, he shared how he vividly remembered the tissue in the toilet, saying, "It was something I will never forget!" To hear him share that memory hurt me because that was the last image we had of our seed. Looking back, I am so grateful for the three sets of ultrasound pictures that are in our keepsake box and have now become a precious emblem to let the world know that even though our precious seed had to be passed that night, her heartbeat still thrives in this world! I remember seeing the paperwork that day at the medical office that said "spontaneous abortion," and it made me angry. I had to ask my friend why they named it that because I did not have an abortion! I miscarried our child. She explained it was a medical term they used in the hospitals and was a normal occurrence. It cut like a glass, but it was something that had been used medically for years. To me, it was just some words on a paper. Nothing could ever take away the powerful and beautiful seed that we created in love and that was birthed in my stomach to carry!

Look Up Dear Child: Finding Strength in God
That week of waiting was a shadow over our home, a dread we couldn't shake. Our precious seed had been my daily companion—her presence felt in every rub of my stomach, every prayer I breathed. I'd speak life over her, claiming John 10:10: "I have come that they may have life, and have it to the full." My husband's hope kept us afloat, his belief that maybe the ultrasound was wrong, that maybe she still lived. He'd fathered two before, and this third child was his dream too. So we waited, honoring his heart, looking up to God for a miracle. Psalm 121:1-2 became my cry: "I lift up my eyes to the mountains—where does my help come from? My help comes from the Lord, the Maker of heaven and earth."

The Verdict and the Storm
The final ultrasound was a verdict—no heartbeat, no hope, just a silent goodbye. The doctor's instructions were mechanical: take the pills, brace for pain. I showered, seeking peace, but the medicine unleashed a storm. The pain was a beast—ripping through me, stealing my breath, drawing screams I didn't know I could make. My first pregnancy, and this was my labor—a cruel mockery with no child to hold. My husband and friend stood by, their presence a comfort but not a cure. I alone bore the task, my body expelling our precious seed in fragments that broke my soul. The medication's side effects doubled the torment—bowels churning, tissue passing, a nightmare unfolding in Route bathroom. Each flush was a farewell, a piece of her lost to necessity. I'd chosen this over a D&C, thinking it gentler, but it was a harrowing I'd never wish on anyone.

God's Power in the Abyss
Time blurred into pain and loss. I ran to the bathroom countless times, my voice gone, my spirit shattered. It was one of the most broken days of my life—a mother's anguish poured out in screams and silence. Yet in that abyss, I looked up. "Look up, dear child," I'd whisper to myself, echoing my own encouragement. Psalm 46:1 roared true: "God is our refuge and strength, an ever-present help in trouble." No one else could carry me—not my husband's tender hands, not my friend's quiet vigil, not even a mother's love. Only God's power lifted me, His might my anchor when all else failed.

A Shared Loss, A Lasting Echo
My husband's memory of that night—the tissue in the toilet—cuts me still. "I'll never forget," he said, his voice a father's lament. For him, this third loss was a quiet wound beside his living children. For me, it was a first, a raw gash in my soul. That shared image binds us, a painful relic of our dear Babygirl. But the ultrasound pictures—three fragile proofs of her heartbeat—are our treasure. They sit in our keepsake box, a testament that she lived, that her rhythm echoes in eternity. Jeremiah 1:5 assures me, "Before I formed you in the womb I knew you." God knew her, loved her, as I did.

Beyond the Label
The term "spontaneous abortion" on the paperwork was a wound of its own. I raged at it, demanded answers. My friend's explanation—medical jargon, not judgment—didn't soften the blow. I didn't choose this; it was taken from me. But labels can't erase our precious seed's truth—conceived in love, carried in faith, lost in sorrow. Romans 8:28 promises, "In all things God works for the good of those who love him." I looked up, trusting He'd weave good from this pain.

Devotional Call to Action: Strength to Say Goodbye
Scripture Reflection: "I lift up my eyes to the mountains—where does my help come from? My help comes from the Lord, the Maker of heaven and earth" (Psalm 121:1-2, NIV).
Meditation: Picture yourself in your darkest moment—passing your child, grieving your loss. Hear God whisper, "Look up, dear child." See Him above you, His strength descending, His arms catching every tear. Your baby is with Him; your help is from Him. Lift your eyes now.
Prayer: Lord, I looked up when I lost my child, and You were there. The pain was unbearable, but Your power carried me. Hold my precious seed in Your arms, and hold me here—heal my heart, steady my soul. Give me strength to trust You still. In Jesus' name, Amen.

Action Steps:

- **Look Up:** Stand or sit, eyes lifted, and say aloud, "My help comes from You, Lord," claiming Psalm 121:2.
- **Write:** Journal about that night or day of loss, ending with "I looked up, and You helped me."
- **Worship:** Sing or listen to "Raise a Hallelujah," letting praise lift your gaze.
- **Honor:** Hold a keepsake of your baby—a photo, a note—and thank God for their life, however brief.
  Encouragement: Dear child, you looked up in distress, and God met you. Your loss broke you, but His strength remade you. Your seed's heartbeat lives in His presence, and you're never alone—look up, He's there.

Chapter 5: The Mother with The Issue Of Blood!

Moving Forward in Silence

Since the baby was no longer in my womb, it was now time to move forward. But how do you move forward when your body still tells a story of pregnancy, a story that ended in silence? How do you embrace a stomach that is still showing like you're pregnant, but in reality had no indication of a child that was coming forth? You take it a day at a time. You grieve knowing that the Father will see you through! After passing Hannah, my womb was empty, but my body lingered in a limbo of loss. My stomach, once a cradle of hope, now bore the weight of absence—a cruel mimicry of the life it once held. In the midst of embracing that trauma, I would hear comments like "You gained a lot of weight!" But the fact of the matter was my body had not healed from the inside out and was showing the effects of regaining any sense of normalcy. Little did people know, I was still bleeding. The miscarriage hadn't released me—it clung to me, a relentless shadow. So, I started having regular visits again to the doctor. But they couldn't explain what was happening. I would hear comments like, "Maybe it's a fibroid." But they weren't sure. Unfortunately, their next step was to give me birth control pills to try and stop the bleeding. That suggestion was a huge mistake and led to an even longer road of recovery.

A Body Betrayed

This had an adverse effect. I would walk up the stairs and lose my breath and have heart palpitations. In addition, I started to have stroke symptoms that included shortness of breath, dizziness, slurred speech, and pains in my face. It's like my face would freeze and my words would not. This went on for six long months. I am attending regular visits, and they still could not offer any answers. Six months of bleeding, of breathlessness, of words slipping away like sand through my fingers—it was a nightmare I couldn't wake from. I'd stand at the sink, trying to ask my husband for help, but my tongue betrayed me, my face locked in a silent plea. I became a mother with an issue of blood—not twelve years like the woman in scripture, but long enough to feel her desperation, her isolation, her cry for wholeness.

A Cry for Healing

I remember the ministry I fellowshipped with at the time had an open call for prayer. I went up because I was tired of the bleeding and symptoms that were related to the illness. My spirit was weary, my body frail, my hope frayed. A lady who had adopted me as her niece—a spiritual auntie whose faith was a beacon—began to boldly profess healing and declared, just like the woman with the issue of blood who reached out and touched the hem of His garment and was made whole, "Heal her body, Father." Her words echoed Matthew 9:20-22, a story I'd clung to in my pain: a woman, bleeding for years, who pressed through a crowd for one touch of Jesus. I left that day feeling peace and believing that the bleeding would stop. It wasn't an instant cure, but a seed of faith planted in my soul, a whisper that I, too, could be made whole.

The Spirit's Revelation

One day, I felt in my spirit to read the effects of the birth control. For some reason, I never threw them away, since I was instructed to take them daily. Low and behold, everything that I had been experiencing in my speech, my face, and my body was written in bold black and white letters on that medication sheet. Heart palpitations, dizziness, slurred speech—it was all there, a catalog of my suffering. I immediately obeyed what I felt in my spirit and shut down the intake of the birth control pills. When I visited the doctor, I shared that every symptom on that paper was what was going on in the last six months. However, the doctor didn't believe me and shared her opinion. But I have learned in my life to listen to the sweet voice of the Holy Spirit. In being obedient and stopping all forms of that medication, not only did the bleeding stop, but all stroke-related symptoms ceased as well. It was a miracle—a mother with an issue of blood, healed not by medicine, but by faith and the Spirit's guidance.

Expanding the Narrative: A Mother's Faith in the Storm

Moving forward after Hannah's loss was like wading through a fog—each step uncertain, each day a reminder of what I'd carried and lost. My stomach, still rounded, was a silent taunt, a physical echo of a pregnancy that had ended. I'd run my hands over it, remembering the prayers I'd whispered, the verses I'd spoken over her. People's careless words—"You gained a lot of weight!"—pierced me, oblivious to the truth: my body was a battlefield, still bleeding, still unhealed. For my husband, with his two children from before, this was a quieter grief, a loss layered atop a life already full. For me, it was a primal wound, a first dream deferred. Yet I took it day by day, leaning on Psalm 147:3: "He heals the brokenhearted and binds up their wounds." God was binding me, slowly, surely.

The Wilderness of Bleeding

The bleeding persisted, a cruel companion to my grief. Doctor visits offered no clarity—only guesses, shrugs, and a prescription for birth control pills. I trusted them at first, desperate to stop the flow, to reclaim my body. But the pills turned traitor. Stairs became a trial, my breath a fleeting ghost, my heart pounding in protest. Then the stroke symptoms struck—dizziness tilting my world, speech faltering, my face a mask of pain. I'd sit, frozen, trying to call out, but my words were lost, my voice a prisoner. Six months of this was a wilderness, a season that made me a mother with an issue of blood—bleeding not just from loss, but from a cure that became a curse. Luke 8:43-44 mirrored my struggle: "And a woman was there who had been subject to bleeding for twelve years… She came up behind him and touched the edge of his cloak, and immediately her bleeding stopped." I wasn't at twelve years, but six months felt eternal.

Pressing Through in Prayer

That prayer call at church was my crowd to press through. I stumbled forward, exhausted, desperate for relief. My spiritual auntie's voice rang out, bold and sure, linking me to that biblical mother. "Heal her, Father," she prayed, claiming my wholeness as Jesus had claimed hers. I didn't feel healed that moment, but peace settled over me—a peace from Philippians 4:7, "which transcends all understanding." It guarded my heart, whispering that my issue of blood had an end. I carried that faith home, a fragile flame against the darkness of my symptoms.

Deliverance by Obedience

The Spirit's nudge to read the pill's side effects was a divine lifeline. I'd kept them, a habit of obedience, and there they sat, unassuming. Unfolding that sheet, I saw my life in print—every symptom a match, a revelation in black and white. The Holy Spirit spoke, clear and sweet: Stop. I obeyed, defying the doctor's doubt. She dismissed me, clinging to her science, but I clung to John 16:13: "When he, the Spirit of truth, comes, he will guide you into all the truth." That truth was my deliverance!

I was a mother with an issue of blood, healed not by man's wisdom, but by God's voice.

Healing Inside Out

This journey was my wilderness, my reaching for the hem. My husband walked beside me, his grief quieter but real. Together, we leaned on a God who heals from the inside out—body, heart, and soul. My stomach flattened, my voice returned, and my spirit lifted, all because I trusted the One who saw me bleed and made me whole.

Devotional Call to Action: Touching the Hem of Healing

Scripture Reflection: "She said to herself, 'If I only touch his cloak, I will be saved.'… Jesus said, 'Daughter, your faith has healed you. Go in peace'" (Matthew 9:21-22, NIV).
Meditation: Imagine yourself as the mother with the issue of blood—your miscarriage's aftermath, your body's struggle, your heart's cry. See yourself pressing through to Jesus, touching His hem. Feel His power stop your bleeding, heal your wounds, and call you "Daughter." Rest in His peace now.
Prayer: Lord, I'm a mother with an issue of blood—bleeding from loss, from pain, from a body that won't heal. I reach for Your hem, trusting Your power to make me whole. Stop my suffering, restore my strength, and speak peace over me. Guide me by Your Spirit, as You did her. In Jesus' name, Amen.

Action Steps:

1. **Reach**: Sit quietly, hands outstretched, and visualize touching Jesus' cloak, claiming healing for your body and soul.

2. **Write**: Journal about a time you felt God's guidance after your loss, pairing it with Matthew 9:22.

3. **Worship**: Listen to "Way Maker," letting the lyrics affirm God's healing touch.

4. **Share**: Tell a trusted friend one way God is healing you, inviting their prayer.
Encouragement: You're a mother, even in loss, and your issue of blood doesn't define you—Jesus does. Reach for Him; your faith brings healing, your pain finds peace. You're whole in His eyes.

Chapter 6: Teleo - It Is Finished!

A Promise of Reunion

I want to highlight a particular passage in the Bible to help see you through. It brings comfort to every parent that even though they lost a child, that baby, who is sinless, goes to heaven. Please be reassured that even though God had other plans for that child, you will one day see them again. "David therefore inquired of God for the child, and David fasted and went and lay all night on the ground. The elders of his household stood beside him in order to raise him up from the ground, but he was unwilling and would not eat food with them. Then it happened on the seventh day that the child died. And the servants of David were afraid to tell him that the child was dead, for they said, 'Behold, while the child was still alive, we spoke to him and he did not listen to our voice. How then can we tell him that the child is dead, since he might do himself harm!' But when David saw that his servants were whispering together, David perceived that the child was dead; so David said to his servants, 'Is the child dead?' And they said, 'He is dead.' So David arose from the ground, washed, anointed himself, and changed his clothes; and he came into the house of the Lord and worshipped. Then he came to his own house, and when he requested, they set food before him and he ate. Then his servants said to him, 'What is this thing you have done? While the child was alive, you fasted and wept; but when the child died, you arose and ate food.' He said, 'While the child was still alive, I fasted and wept; for I said, "Who knows, the Lord may be gracious to me, that the child may live." But now he has died; why should I fast? Can I bring him back again? I will go to him, but he will not return to me.'" (2 Samuel 12:16-23).

A Foundation of Strength

So, know that your sweet seed is resting in the arms of the Lord. Holding on to that promise will allow you to have a solid foundation to stand on. It will keep you strengthened even in the processes when you don't understand. It allows you to hold on to the word of God in the midst of the pain. But most importantly, it gives you a security in Him, that no matter what, He is there to carry you through every part of it!

Expanding the Narrative: Teleo - It Is Finished!

After the bleeding stopped, after my body ceased its rebellion, there came a quiet—a stillness that was both relief and reckoning. Hannah was gone from my womb, her brief life finished here, yet her absence left a void that echoed with questions. "Teleo," Jesus said on the cross in John 19:30—"It is finished." That word, that declaration of completion, began to resonate in my spirit. My suffering, my loss, my Hannah's journey on earth—it was finished, not abandoned, not wasted, but brought to a divine end. Yet how do you live with that ending? How do you walk forward when your arms are empty, when your heart still beats for a child who no longer does? The answer came in a scripture that wrapped around my soul like a balm: 2 Samuel 12:16-23, the story of David and his lost son.

David's Mirror of Grief

David's story became my mirror. He, too, had carried a child in hope—a son born to Bathsheba, a fragile life hanging in the balance. He inquired of God, fasted, lay on the ground all night, pleading for mercy. I understood that desperation. I'd rubbed my stomach, prayed Psalm 139:13—"For you created my inmost being; you knit me together in my mother's womb"—and begged God to let Hannah live. David's elders watched him, just as my husband and friend watched me, helpless yet present. Then, on the seventh day, David's child died. The servants whispered, fearing his reaction, just as I'd feared the ultrasound's silence, the doctor's words. But David perceived the truth—"Is the child dead?" "He is dead." And then, something extraordinary: he arose, washed, anointed himself, changed his clothes, and worshipped. He ate, he lived, he moved forward. His servants were baffled, but his words cut through my grief: "I will go to him, but he will not return to me."

Hope Beyond the Pain

For me, Hannah's passing was a night of screams, a blur of pain, a flushing away of dreams. For my husband, it was a quieter sorrow, a third child lost beside the two he still held. But David's response became our hope. "Teleo"—it was finished here, but not forever. Hannah, sinless and pure, was in heaven, resting in the arms of the Lord. That truth didn't erase the ache—it gave it purpose. I couldn't bring her back, no amount of fasting or weeping could undo the miscarriage, but I could go to her. One day, I'd see her face, hear her laugh, hold her hand. Revelation 21:4 painted the picture: "He will wipe every tear from their eyes. There will be no more death or mourning or crying or pain, for the old order of things has passed away." Teleo—the old order of pain was finished; a new order of reunion awaited.

Healing and Clarity

Holding this promise became my foundation. After six months of bleeding, of stroke-like symptoms, of a body that wouldn't heal, I'd found wholeness through the Holy Spirit's guidance. But the emotional healing lingered, a slower mending. People didn't see that—they saw my still-swollen stomach, my exhaustion, and judged. "You've gained weight," they'd say, unaware of the war I'd fought. My husband saw deeper, his eyes tracing the lines of my grief, his own heart echoing mine. We'd lost Hannah together, yet our paths diverged—his tempered by fatherhood's joys, mine raw with its absence. Yet 2 Samuel 12:23 steadied us both: she was safe, and we'd go to her. That assurance strengthened me when I didn't understand—why her, why now, why this way? It let me cling to God's word when pain roared loudest. Matthew 19:14 echoed, "Let the little children come to me, and do not hinder them, for the kingdom of heaven belongs to such as these." Hannah was with Jesus, unhindered, whole.

Security in His Presence

Most importantly, this promise gave me security in Him. No matter the loss, the questions, the lingering scars, He carried me through every part. The night I passed her, I'd looked up, and He'd held me. The months of bleeding, He'd guided me. Now, in the aftermath, He anchored me. Psalm 23:4 became my song: "Even though I walk through the darkest valley, I will fear no evil, for you are with me." Teleo—it was finished, not with despair, but with hope. Hannah's life, brief as a breath, was complete in heaven, and I could rest in that truth. My husband and I could walk forward, not forgetting, but trusting—our sweet seed was in the arms of the Lord, and we'd meet her again.

Deepening the Reflection: A Finished Work

David's worship after loss stunned me. How could he rise, wash, anoint himself, and praise? Yet I saw it—his child was finished here, but safe with God. I'd worshipped too, in my way—through tears, through prayers, through obedience to the Spirit. After Hannah's passing, I'd clung to those ultrasound pictures, three fragile proofs of her heartbeat. They weren't just memories; they were declarations that her life mattered, that it wasn't unfinished in God's eyes. "Teleo" didn't mean abandonment—it meant fulfillment. John 19:30 wasn't just Jesus' cry; it was Hannah's story too—her purpose complete, her place secure.

Reframing the Pain

This chapter isn't about erasing pain—it's about reframing it. The bleeding, the symptoms, the miscarriage—they were finished, but so was my despair. God had other plans for Hannah, plans I couldn't see, but plans sealed with love. Jeremiah 29:11 promised, "For I know the plans I have for you… plans to give you hope and a future." Her future was heaven; mine was to carry on, to heal, to hope. My husband's quiet strength beside me, his memory of her tissue a shared wound, reminded me we weren't alone. We'd go to her together, one day, a family reunited beyond the veil.

A Rock of Assurance

So, dear reader, know your sweet seed is resting in His arms. Whether your loss was early or late, whether you held them or only dreamed of them, they're safe. Teleo—it is finished here, but not forever. Hold that promise; let it be your rock, your strength, your security. God carries you through every part, whispering, "You will go to them."

Devotional Call to Action: Resting in "Teleo"

Scripture Reflection: "I will go to him, but he will not return to me" (2 Samuel 12:23, NIV); "It is finished" (John 19:30, NIV).

Meditation: Picture your child in Jesus' arms—sinless, safe, whole. Hear Him say, "Teleo—it is finished." Your loss is complete here, but their life thrives in heaven. See yourself one day running to them, tears wiped away. Rest in that finished work now.

Prayer: Lord, my sweet seed is with You, and I trust Your arms around them. "Teleo"—it's finished here, but not forever. Comfort me with the promise I'll go to them. Strengthen me to stand, heal me to hope, carry me through this pain. In Jesus' name, Amen.

Action Steps:

1. **Visualize**: Close your eyes and imagine your child with Jesus, smiling, waiting for you.

2. **Write**: Journal a letter to your baby, ending with "I'll go to you," and pair it with 2 Samuel 12:23.

3. **Worship**: Sing or listen to "It Is Finished" by Bethel Music, letting "Teleo" sink deep.

4. **Share**: Tell a loved one your child's name or a memory, affirming their place in heaven.
   Encouragement: Your loss is finished, but your child's story isn't—they're with Him, and you'll go to them. Teleo seals your pain with hope; stand on that promise today.

Chapter 7: The Miscarriage Is Not the Marriage!

A Vow Tested

Even through the heartache, even through the disdain, we could not let it break our bond! Because in our vows we professed openly in front of our loved ones, "Through sickness and health, till death do us part." Our situation felt like a death sentence! One minute we were welcoming being parents with open arms. The next moment we were looking at an ultrasound machine that was dark and covered with blood, trying to figure out how to share the news with our loved ones. We were learning that life would drastically change in an instant. That your world could be turned upside down and you have absolutely zero control of the situation. Hannah's loss wasn't just a miscarriage—it was a seismic shift, a rupture in the joy we'd built together. My husband, already a father to two, felt the sting differently, his grief tempered by the children he still held. For me, it was my first—a dream extinguished before it could dawn. Yet through the tears, through the silence, we clung to our vows, refusing to let this death sentence sever us.

A Still Small Voice

The amazing thing is that through this trial, there was a still small voice that let us know that we were not alone. The Bible says in Psalm 46:1, "God is our refuge and strength, he is a very present help in a time of trouble." This means He is in the midst of the situation we are facing. So, if you are a person, be it a male or a female, who lost a child, God is there! He understands where you are, and what you feel. It is fine to be sad, angry, to talk to people who genuinely care about your well-being, to cry on your significant other's shoulders, to take time to heal, but most importantly. to ask questions. Here are a few questions and biblical solutions that may help you process the grief:

1. **How do I release the hurt from losing a child?**
   Surrender everything attached to it! To surrender in Strong's Concordance (3860) is the Greek word paradidomi (pronounced par-ad-id-o-mee), which means to yield up, entrust, transmit—bring forth, cast, commit, deliver (up), give (over, up). The Bible says in 1 Peter 5:7 to, "Cast all your cares on the Lord, for he careth for you!" Let this scripture be a catalyst for your healing from losing a child.

2. **What do I do when people say insensitive comments, even though it may be their own personal way of offering comfort?**
   Prioritize your own emotional well-being. If you hear a comment like, "You can always have another baby," you may say something like, "That's a difficult thing to say right now, as I'm still grieving the loss of our baby!" Another response is, "I appreciate you trying to comfort me, but comments of that nature make it harder." The key is to respond with kindness. There is a famous quote by Boyd Bailey

that goes, "Kindness benefits everyone. It brings joy to the giver and peace to the receiver." In addition, a biblical scripture can be found in Romans 2:4, which tells us that God's kindness leads people to repentance. So, your act of love, through your response, is a humble demonstration of a seed that is being planted. That word you shared to the person, through your own pain and discomfort, can one day blossom into faith in Christ. This allows you to show God's love in practical ways.

3. **How do you convey to close loved ones, family, and friends that the baby is no longer here?**
Express trust in God's plan: Convey in a timely manner that is comfortable for you and your spouse. A simple way to express what happened is, "We wanted to share with you that we lost the baby, but are working through the trial. We know that God had other plans for our baby and we appreciate your love, support, and prayers that have been shared." A powerful scripture to stand on is found in Revelation 21:4, "Though we grieve deeply, we hold onto the promise that God will wipe away every tear." Remember the word of God is a sense of encouragement, meant to edify your spirit.

4. **How can we heal as a couple?**
Embrace the process: First, be reassured that God is with the both of you! He is the ONLY one who can bring "beauty for ashes," as outlined in Isaiah 61:3, which means even in times of great hardship, loss, or grief, God can bring forth something beautiful and positive from the ashes in your lives, essentially transforming your pain into something meaningful and hopeful. So no matter how hard it is to express yourself, know at the appointed time God will take you through healing so you can be transformed through your heart, mind, and spirit. It is key to know that ashes are a symbol of mourning, but within the loss, He can make it one of the most beautiful experiences if you yield to His will.

5. **How can we be fine if our future does not involve another child of our own?**
Accept God's purpose and plan for your life. This means placing your focus on trusting that God has a unique purpose for your life, even without biological children. I had to come to a place of peace and rest and embrace the many children that God has placed under my tutelage for the past thirty-five years. This process takes time, so you must give yourself grace through it and have trust in the Father that He will see you through it. Other tools include praying through your desires and pain, finding comfort in the stories of biblical figures who also faced childlessness; most importantly, remembering that God's plan might not always align with our expectations, but it is still good and loving.

6a). **Healing and Clarity: How do you trust God after losing a child?**
The first step is to acknowledge your pain. It is imperative to not lean to your own understanding, but to the Lord for healing and understanding. Acknowledging your anger, confusion, and even resentment is key to learning to trust the Lord again. Don't be afraid to direct your questions to the Father, so He can mend your heartstrings and put your life back together again. God is able to handle your grief because He created you in His image. Meditate on Psalm 34:18, which states, "The Lord is close to the brokenhearted; He rescues those whose spirits are crushed." He's with those who belong to Him who experience hardship and suffering, whose hearts are crushed by the tragedies and discords of life.

6b). **You Must Rest in Him!**
Although you may not fully understand His ways, you must trust His good nature. So, whatever you are going through, rest in God's goodness. The biblical significance of rest is found in the below connotations:
• Rest is a gift from God
• Rest is sacred
• Being free from guilt and worry (The loss is not your fault!)
• Drawing closer to God
• Rest is a funnel for grace (We find security, mercy, and unconditional love through Him!)
• Rest restores and brings balance to our lives
• Practicing contentment and gratitude
• Setting boundaries
• Releasing worries
• Rest helps us to refocus on what's more important

Instead of questioning the Father, trust Him to bring clarity through your pain and sadness and let Him comfort you through it all. He will remain close to your broken heart! He is the KEY to your wholeness.

7. **How do I manage Mother's Day, which is a constant reminder of the baby?**
The key is you can't manage Mother's Day because the emotions will come and it is a constant reminder that you lost the child. So, the answer is to "Lean to Him, the author and finisher of your faith, to carry you through the day." Ask the Lord to guide you, to give you rest and peace as you navigate through the day, to help you stay positive and to guard your heart from negative thoughts that may try to boost their ugly heads. Remember, it is not our will, but His will. We are not in control; He is the one guiding the boat. So, if you lean to the Father, HE will carry you through!

As you take the time to meditate openly and honestly, you will find yourself in various stages of your healing journey.

A Bond Unbroken

The miscarriage wasn't just Hannah's loss—it was ours, a shared wound that tested the vows we'd spoken with such certainty. "Through sickness and health, till death do us part"—words that once felt romantic now bore the weight of reality. That dark ultrasound screen, the blood where life should have been, felt like a death sentence, a guillotine slicing through our joy. One moment, we'd laughed, dreamed, planned—my husband envisioning a third child to join his two, me cradling my first. The next, we sat in silence, grappling with how to tell our loved ones that our world had flipped upside down. Control slipped through our fingers like sand, leaving us raw, exposed, and clinging to each other.

God's Presence in the Chaos

Yet in that chaos, a still small voice whispered, as it did to Elijah in 1 Kings 19:12—God's presence, steady and sure. Psalm 46:1 became our lifeline: "God is our refuge and strength, a very present help in trouble." He was there, in the doctor's office, in our quiet car ride home, in the nights we cried together. My husband's grief was quieter, softened by his other children, but no less real. I felt the void more keenly, an emptiness where motherhood should have begun. Yet God understood us both—male and female, husband and wife—and met us where we stood. It was okay to be angry, to sob on his shoulder, to ask why. And through those questions, we found answers—not to end the pain, but to endure it together.

Surrendering the Pain

Surrendering the hurt was my first step. Paradidomi—to yield up, to cast—I gave it all to God, as 1 Peter 5:7 urged. The guilt, the what-ifs, the ache of Hannah's absence—I laid them at His feet. My husband did too, in his way, his steady faith a rock I leaned on. When people said, "You can have another," I'd bristle, but kindness became my shield. "I'm still grieving," I'd say, planting seeds of grace, as Romans 2:4 promised. Telling our families was harder—we waited, then spoke: "We lost her, but God has her." Revelation 21:4 held us—"He will wipe away every tear"—a promise we shared through tears of our own.

Healing as a Couple

Healing as a couple meant embracing the ashes. Isaiah 61:3 was our vow renewed—beauty for ashes, God's gift to us both. We talked, we prayed, we sat in silence, letting Him transform our pain. My husband's strength bolstered me; my vulnerability softened him. What if no more children came? I'd taught children for thirty-five years—God's purpose unfolded there, a grace I grew into. Trusting Him again meant owning our pain—my anger, his quiet resolve—and letting Psalm 34:18 mend us: "The Lord is close to the brokenhearted." Rest became our refuge—no guilt, just His goodness, as Matthew 11:28 invited: "Come to me… and I will give you rest."

Facing Mother's Day

Mother's Day loomed, a dagger to my heart. I couldn't manage it—the emotions flooded, unbidden. So I leaned on Him, the author and finisher (Hebrews 12:2), asking for peace. My husband held me, his presence a silent prayer, and together we navigated the day, trusting God's will over ours. The miscarriage wasn't our marriage—it was a chapter, not the book. We'd vowed to endure, and with Him, we would.

Devotional Call to Action: Healing Together in Him

Scripture Reflection: "God is our refuge and strength, a very present help in trouble" (Psalm 46:1, NIV).
Meditation: Picture you and your spouse in God's refuge—your miscarriage's pain between you, His strength around you. See Him binding your bond, turning ashes to beauty. Feel His presence as your help, your healer, your hope. Rest in Him together now.
Prayer: Lord, our miscarriage shook us, but it won't break us. You're our refuge, our strength. Hold us close—heal our hurts, mend our marriage, transform our ashes. Guide us to surrender, trust, and rest in You. Carry us through, together. In Jesus' name, Amen.

Action Steps:

1. **Surrender**: Sit with your spouse, name one hurt from your loss, and pray 1 Peter 5:7 together, casting it to God.

2. **Write**: Journal a kind response to an insensitive comment, planting a seed of grace with Romans 2:4.

3. **Worship**: Sing "Beauty for Ashes" by Chris McClarney, letting it renew your hope as a couple.

4. **Rest**: Share one way God's been present, then rest in silence, trusting His plan. **Encouragement**: Your miscarriage isn't your marriage—God is your bond's keeper. Lean on Him, lean on each other; He'll carry you through every tear to beauty anew.

Chapter 8: The Elephant In The Room

Facing the Elephant Head-On

Miscarriage was the elephant in the room—an uninvited guest that loomed large, silent, and heavy. When our precious seed slipped away, I stepped into a world where her absence was a secret no one dared whisper. Society saw no child in my arms, so they saw no loss. But to me, to my husband, she was real—our seed, our promise, our prayer answered in the fall of two thousand and eighteen. My husband grinning at the thought of a third, me marveling at my first. Then in a split moment—she was gone! Our world didn't just shift—it shattered. We were left to gather the fragments, to learn how to breathe again in a life that no longer fit.

The Crushing Silence
That silence crushed us. People didn't ask, didn't speak her name, as if she'd never existed. But she mattered—her brief life carved into our souls. The elephant grew, its weight pressing on every conversation we avoided, every baby item we hid. My husband felt it too, his grief quieter but no less deep. His two children from before were a balm, but our precious seed's loss was a wound he carried beside me. We couldn't pretend she hadn't been real—not when I'd felt her grow, not when we'd heard her heartbeat thump through that machine. To ignore her was to bury a piece of us, and I refused to let that beast win.

Confronting the Beast
So I faced it—the ugly, hulking elephant of miscarriage. It's okay to talk about it, to scream her name, to weep into that tiny outfit I'd bought. I'd let go of the vision of the nursery, not to forget, but to heal, each release a step toward inner peace. Brushing it under the rug wasn't an option. I'd seen the cost in my own heart—those early days when silence bred bitterness, when I'd flinch at strollers, resent my husband's calm, or question God's goodness. Left unchecked, that elephant could trample us into regret, rage, even despair. Proverbs 14:30 warned, "A heart at peace gives life to the body, but envy rots the bones." I wouldn't let it rot us—we had to speak, to grieve, to live again.

Strength in God's Presence
God met me when I asked for strength. That "spontaneous abortion" label on the paperwork was a dagger—clinical, cold, wrong. I didn't choose this; it was thrust upon me. My friend's explanation—medical jargon—didn't dull the sting, but it forced me to confront the elephant. Our precious seed wasn't just words on a page; she was our love made flesh, a seed I'd carried with joy. Asking why, demanding answers, was my rebellion against the silence. And God answered—not with platitudes, but with presence. Psalm 34:18 became my lifeline: "The Lord is close to the brokenhearted and saves those who are crushed in spirit." He was close when I stood alone, waiting for whispers that didn't come, when other women's "I lost a child" hung in the air, unfinished.

Hunger for Healing
Those brief comments from others—half-spoken, quickly dropped—left me hungry. I needed more, craved stories to stitch my healing. But the world stayed mute, and I stood in the stillness, day and night, aching for clarity. Then, when my heart was ready—when my husband's was too—God moved. Malachi 3:10 promised, "See if I will not throw open the floodgates of heaven and pour out so much blessing that there will not be room enough to store it." He did. Answers rained down—not full explanations, but revelations of His love, His purpose, His nearness. It was surgery on our souls—painful, precise, redemptive. My husband and I wept, held each other, and found our precious seed's place in eternity. The elephant shrank, its shadow lifting as God gave us what we'd sought: not just closure, but courage to speak her name.

Devotional Call to Action: Naming the Elephant
Scripture Reflection: "The Lord is close to the brokenhearted and saves those who are crushed in spirit" (Psalm 34:18, NIV).
Meditation: Picture the elephant in your room—your miscarriage, silent and heavy. See God step in, closer than your breath, lifting its weight. Name your loss, speak your child's name, and feel Him save your crushed spirit. He's here, now, with you.
Prayer: Father, my miscarriage is an elephant I've hidden, but You see it. Be close to my broken heart—save me from silence, bitterness, despair. Give me strength to face it, to speak it, to heal. Hold my sweet seed and me together in Your love. In Jesus' name, Amen.

Action Steps:

- **Speak:** Say your child's name aloud, alone or with your spouse, affirming their reality.
- **Write:** Journal about the "elephant"—what you've avoided—and pair it with Psalm 34:18.
- **Worship:** Sing "Reckless Love," letting God's nearness drown the silence.
- **Share:** Tell one person your story, breaking the secret, trusting God's strength.
  Encouragement: The elephant doesn't own you—God does. Your baby mattered, your grief matters. Face it with Him; He's close, saving, healing. Speak, and let the floodgates open.

Chapter 9: Weeping Endures for A Night, But Joy Cometh in The Morning

A Long Night of Tears

The weeping had lasted far longer than a night—months of tears, of silence, of a stomach that no longer held our precious seed's life. My husband and I had walked through the valley, his grief a steady shadow to my raw anguish. He had his two children, a tether to fatherhood I couldn't claim, yet our precious seed's loss bound us in a shared sorrow. That weekend at the prophetic event, though, was a turning point—a dawn breaking through our darkness. I was backstage, bustling with tasks, but my heart stayed with him. Marriage had taught me to lift him up, even in my busyness, so I whispered a prayer: "Lord, care for him. Let Your word find him." I trusted Psalm 46:1—"God is our refuge and strength, a very present help in trouble"—knowing He'd be near us both.

A Prophet's Revelation
God didn't just answer—He astonished us. My husband's eyes sparkled as he ran to me, words tumbling out: "A prophet approached me!" The prophet saw beyond the visible—past his two living children to the third, our precious seed, a girl lost to miscarriage. For months, I'd wondered—was she a daughter, a son? That unanswered question gnawed at me, a hole in my healing. In that moment, God filled it, proving He's near in our need. My husband, steady and strong, felt the weight of her too—a third child he'd never hold here. The prophet's words were a gift, a revelation that stitched a piece of our brokenness back together.

A Name of Grace
That night, I stood in the shower, water mingling with tears. I rubbed my empty stomach, a ritual of grief, and cried out, "Lord, what did You name her?" His voice—soft, sure—whispered, "Hannah, which represents my grace." The name sank deep, a balm to my soul. In His sovereignty, God had chosen her, planted her in me to release grace—not just for us, but for the world. Names carry destiny, purpose etched in every syllable. Her name wasn't random; it was a declaration of healing, a legacy of mending broken hearts. Psalm 30:5 sang true: "Weeping may endure for a night, but joy comes in the morning." The night of loss stretched long, but joy dawned with her name.

Beauty for Ashes
Isaiah 61:3 became our exchange—beauty for ashes, a crown for mourning, praise for despair. God didn't just comfort us; He transformed us. The ashes of our precious seed's loss—shame at my body's failure, disgrace in silence, grief's heavy cloak—were traded for beauty. Her brief life wasn't a waste; it was a purpose fulfilled in heaven, a grace that rippled outward. My husband and I held this promise together, his quiet faith bolstering my fragile hope. The prophet's word, her name, her gender—they were God's tender mercies, proof He cares for the little things. Matthew 10:30 says, "Even the very

hairs of your head are all numbered." If He counts hairs, He surely counts tears, names babies, heals hearts.

Redemption's Joy
This joy wasn't the absence of pain—it was redemption through it. Our precious seed's loss had crushed us, but God mended us—our hearts, our marriage, our future. He opened our minds to see newness, a direction beyond the storm. Jeremiah 29:11 echoed, "I know the plans I have for you… plans to give you hope and a future." Her purpose wasn't erased; it was eternal. My husband and I stood taller, not forgetting, but rejoicing—she served a divine role, and we'd see her again. The morning had come, and with it, mounds of joy.

Deepening the Reflection: Joy's Redemptive Power
That prophetic moment was a lifeline—God's hand reaching into our night. The weeping had been relentless—the ultrasound's silence, the pain of passing her, the months of wondering. Yet joy came, not as a denial of loss, but as its fulfillment. Her name, her girlhood, her grace—they were God's surgery on our souls, cutting away despair to plant hope. Isaiah 61:3 wasn't just a verse; it was our story—ashes of grief swapped for a crown of beauty, a garment of praise lifting the heaviness. My husband's awe at the prophet's insight, my tears in the shower—they wove us closer, a shared joy in her eternal place.

A Promise for the Broken
If you've lost a seed, know this: God waits to trade your ashes for beauty. Your night of weeping has an end—joy comes, not to erase, but to redeem. He heals your heart, mends your bonds, and catapults you forward. Your child's purpose isn't lost; it's held in His hands, a grace for you and others. Our precious seed's morning broke our dawn—yours is coming too.

Devotional Call to Action: Embracing Morning Joy
Scripture Reflection: "Weeping may stay for the night, but rejoicing comes in the morning" (Psalm 30:5, NIV); "To provide for those who grieve… beauty instead of ashes" (Isaiah 61:3, NIV).
Meditation: Picture your night of weeping—your loss, your tears. See the dawn breaking, God handing you beauty for ashes, joy for sorrow. Hear Him name your child, affirm their purpose. Feel the morning light warm your heart. Step into His joy now.
Prayer: Lord, my weeping has been long, but You promise joy. Trade my ashes for beauty, my despair for praise. Name my child in Your grace, heal my heart with their purpose. Bring my morning—restore me, renew me, carry me to hope. In Jesus' name, Amen.

Action Steps:

- **Ask:** Pray, "Lord, what's my child's name?" Write what you hear, trusting His care.
- **Exchange:** List one ash of your loss, then claim Isaiah 61:3's beauty over it.
- **Worship:** Sing "Goodness of God," letting joy rise from your night.
- **Hope:** Share with your spouse or a friend one way God's bringing your morning.
  Encouragement: Your night ends—joy comes. Your seed's purpose lives in Him, and He's crafting beauty from your ashes. Embrace the morning; He's waiting with grace.

Chapter 10: A Father's Silent Funeral Saying Goodbye in the Bathroom

The Silence, the Pain, and the Healing

Hello, my name is Richard L. Holbert, and I'm Hannah's dad. That sentence alone holds more weight than I can explain. Because for years, I've carried the reality of those words in silence. Six years ago, I stood in our bathroom, watching my wife labor through the loss of our daughter. The silence that followed was deafening—her screams fading, my voice trapped. I flushed Hannah away, a funeral without tears, without words, because I had to be strong.

A Rock in the Storm

My wife's world crumbled—she'd carried our beginning, our hope—and I became the rock, burying my pain to hold her up. I knew I should have wept. I should have grieved. I should have allowed myself to feel the weight of the loss, but I didn't. Instead, I did what I thought a husband was supposed to do—what a father was supposed to do. I held everything in. I became the pillar, the steady one, the strong one. And yet, the loss never left me.

A Hidden Grief

My two kids from before gave me a father's title, but Hannah's absence carved a void no legacy could fill. Sometimes feeling it so deeply that it takes the breath out of me, and other times suppressing it so much that it was as if it never even happened. For a long time, I didn't cry. Not because I didn't want to, but because I couldn't. My wife needed me. I had to be strong. I had to be the foundation when our world cracked beneath us. There was no space for my sorrow, no room for my pain. So, I buried it.

Shadows of Loss

That grief didn't leave—it hid, a shadow in every milestone. Father's Day brought no third card, just a pang I ignored. Christmas silence mocked me—no laughter, just echoes of what might've been. Quiet nights haunted me—visions of her hands, her steps, her "Daddy"—and I shoved them down. Men don't get pain's luxury, right? I mastered forgetting, living 98% like she never was. But that 2%—it stole my breath, a silent ache I couldn't name. Fear fueled it too—fear of another loss, of my wife's eyes dimming again. I'd heard tales of repeated heartbreak; I couldn't risk her. Hope was a minefield, so I sidestepped it, never broaching "trying again." Silence felt safer than words.

Fear of Hope

Because deep down, there was fear. Not just fear of grieving, but fear of trying again. What if it happened again? What if the loss repeated itself? I had heard the stories—stories of women who suffered miscarriage after miscarriage before ever carrying a child to term. And I wasn't sure I could survive watching my wife go through that. I wasn't sure she could pull through the thoughts or loss of another child. I didn't want to put her through that kind of pain again. I couldn't. I had seen how much this broke her. I had watched the way the joy in her eyes dimmed after we lost Hannah. The hope, the excitement—only to be crushed by devastation. So, I avoided the conversation.

Burying the Pain

I already knew what my heart was saying. I didn't want to hope. Hope was dangerous. Hope meant reopening wounds I had worked so hard to close. Hope meant risking another heartbreak. Hope meant remembering. And I had spent too long forgetting.

Unspoken Sorrow

I was sad. I was angry. I was hurt. But I never showed it. And the most difficult part? I had suppressed it for so long that I had failed to even ask God to help me. I prayed for other things—protection, guidance. I prayed for my wife, for our marriage, for our future. But it never dawned on me to pray about this. I never asked God to heal me from this wound because I had buried it so deep, I had convinced myself I didn't need healing. But I did.

The Silent Funeral

And the hardest moment of all? The last time I saw my daughter, she wasn't in a photo. There was no ultrasound I could hold onto. My wife and I made the decision to let her pass naturally. She labored, just as if she was giving birth. And when it was over—my daughter was in the toilet. And I flushed her down. That was my funeral. That was my goodbye. That was my only moment of release, and even in that, I had to hold it in. No little hands would ever reach up for me. No tiny feet would stumble as I helped her take her first steps. No small voice would look up at me and say, "I love you, Daddy." She was here. We were excited. And then—a heartbeat was gone. And she was gone.

Breaking the Silence

And how was I supposed to explain to anyone what that felt like? How do you tell another man, "I'm hurting because I lost my child?" Men don't talk like that. They tell each other, "Man up." I was down, drowning in suppressed sorrow, until faith cracked me open. Psalm 147:3 whispered, "He heals the brokenhearted and binds up their wounds." Spirit Life Church and Revelation Church LA showed me God wasn't done—my setback was His set-up. Healing's a journey, not a word—a choice to face pain.

Healing Through Honesty

But here's what I've learned. Healing begins with honesty. I had to talk to God about it. I had to talk to my wife about it. And then, I had to talk to you. Because now I understand that my pain wasn't meant to stay locked inside me. It was meant to be used to help others heal.

A Purpose Shared

I spoke—to God, "Heal me"; to my wife, tears falling; now to you. Silence wasn't strength; honesty is. Hannah's loss isn't buried, it's a purpose to share, a wound to heal others. I'm not whole, but I'm healing, step by step, for her, for us, for every dad who's flushed a dream away.

Devotional Call to Action: Releasing the Silent Funeral

Scripture Reflection: "He heals the brokenhearted and binds up their wounds" (Psalm 147:3, NIV).
Meditation: Picture that bathroom or the place you lost your child—your child's goodbye, your silent funeral. See God there, catching your unshed tears. Feel Him lift the weight you've buried, binding your wounds. Release it to Him now—your pain has a place.
Prayer: *Lord, I'm my child's dad, and I've buried their loss in silence. It's heavy—heal my broken heart, bind my wounds. Take this silent funeral, give me strength to grieve, to speak, to hope. Be my rock. In Jesus' name, Amen.*

Action Steps:

1. **Name It**: Say your child's name aloud, honoring their place in your heart.
2. **Write**: Journal that hardest moment—the goodbye—and pair it with Psalm 147:3.
3. **Worship**: Sing "What a Friend We Have in Jesus," letting your pain flow to Him.
4. **Talk**: Tell your wife or a friend one feeling you've suppressed, breaking the silence.
   Encouragement: Dad, your funeral doesn't define you—God does. You're not down; He's lifting you. Grieve, heal, trust—He's binding your wounds with love.

Chapter 11: Man to Man: Man Down

A Father's Cry Heard

I'm Richard L. Holbert, and I've been down—man down—since losing Hannah six years ago. Fathers, this is for you—the ones who've stood silent while your wives wept, who've carried miscarriage's weight without a word. That night in the bathroom, I watched my daughter pass—and locked my pain in a vault. I had two kids already—living proof I was a dad—but Hannah was ours, a dream we'd named, a heartbeat we'd heard. We'd sat together, my wife and I, my strong hand on her belly, my voice steady with excitement. Society doesn't see our loss—no child to show, no proof—but we feel it, a dagger in our chests, a weight we bear alone, sharp and cold, cutting through every pretense of strength.

The Silent Burden

Men don't talk about this. We're told to fix it, to be the rock. I tried—God, I tried. When that ultrasound went dark, blood where life should've been, I held my wife's hand, steadied her as she shattered. Her first child—her everything—gone in a blink. My grief stayed mute, a shadow to her cries, a quiet ache I wouldn't let surface. I suppressed it, thinking strength meant silence, that my role was to bear it so she could break. Father's Day rolled around, and I smiled for my two, their hugs warm, their cards bright—but Hannah's absence cut deeper than I'd admit, a silent stab I masked with a nod. Birthdays, holidays—her spirit lingered in every quiet corner, every empty chair at the table, every unopened gift I'd imagined for her. I'd see her in my mind—tiny hands reaching, feet stumbling toward me, calling in a voice I'd never hear—and I'd push it down, hard, fast, deep. It floored me, a man down with no one to tell, no words to shape the hurt.

Faith's Breaking Point

God saw me when I couldn't see myself—saw the man beneath the mask. Psalm 34:18 says, "The Lord is close to the brokenhearted and saves those who are crushed in spirit." I was broken—spirit, soul, body—every part of me splintered, and He waited, patient, steady. Spirit Life Church and Revelation Church LA broke through my walls, showed me faith isn't just pews and hymns; it's trust when you're flat on your face, when your knees hit the floor and your voice cracks. I'd thought God failed me—left me in that bathroom, alone with the flush. He was setting me up, not for punishment, but purpose, a plan I couldn't see through the tears I wouldn't shed. Healing's a fight, a daily grind to face the hurt I'd buried under layers of "I'm fine." I talked to Him—finally—about Hannah. "Why her? Why me? Why this way?" My voice shook, fists clenched, questions spilling out after years of quiet. He didn't explain; He held me, close as breath, His presence a balm I hadn't known I needed. Then I talked to my wife—tears fell, words stumbled out like baby birds with broken wings, and the dome cracked open, spilling six years of silence. She'd carried Hannah's body; I'd lugged her pain in my stillness. We grieved together—her sobs, my whispers—man down no more, rising as one.

Man to Man: You're Not Alone

Man to man, I get it—you're down too, aren't you? Your wife's pain is loud, a wail that fills the room; yours is a whisper, a low hum you've muffled. You've buried it—maybe in work, clocking overtime to outrun it; maybe in silence, nodding through the days; maybe in "being strong," shoulders squared against the ache. Maybe you've got other kids, a shield like mine, their laughter a bittersweet buffer, or maybe this was your first, a dream snatched away before you could cradle it. Either way, you don't have to stay down—hear me, you don't. Lamentations 3:22-23 promises, "Because of the Lord's great love we are not consumed, for his compassions never fail. They are new every morning." Your loss isn't your end—it's a wound God can heal, a scar He can redeem. I've learned to grieve—not just for her, my wife, but for me, the dad who lost his girl. I've learned to hope—not recklessly, not with blind leaps, but in Him, steady and sure. And I've learned to talk—man to man, father to father—because your pain's got a purpose too, a story that can lift another.

Rising with Purpose

You're not weak for feeling this—I wasn't, though I thought I was. That bathroom, that flush, that blood—it's okay to hurt, to let it hit you. I avoided hope, feared it like a storm, but God's compassion renewed me, morning by morning, tear by tear. When you're ready—when the weight gets too heavy—talk. Talk to Him, spill it out, raw and real; talk to her, let her see your cracks; talk to me, or any man who'll listen. When you ask, "How do I get up?" I'll say, "Tell me what's down there—what's crushing you?" When you wonder, "How do I help her?" I'll listen, not judge, not fix—just hear you. When you admit, "I'm down," I'll point you to Him—He's close, saving, lifting, His love a lifeline. Healing's not suppressing—it's sharing, letting the vault break, letting the pain breathe. My daughter's funeral was a flush, a cold goodbye in a bathroom, but my healing's a journey—slow, messy, real. You're not alone, man—God's here, closer than you know; I'm here, a father who's been down too. Let's get up together, step by step, from man down to man restored—restored in Him, for her, for us.

Deepening the Reflection: Rising with Purpose

Six years of silence taught me this: burying pain doesn't kill it—it festers, grows roots, chokes you from the inside. Hannah's loss was my wife's first, my third, but it was ours—ours to carry, ours to mourn, a shared wound we navigated in different ways. I'd mastered "man up," squared my shoulders, set my jaw—but "man down" was truer, a reality I couldn't outrun. Faith flipped that script—God didn't leave me down there in the dirt; He lifted me, one hand at a time. Psalm 30:5 says, "Weeping may stay for the night, but rejoicing comes in the morning." My night was long—years of suppressed tears, of bathroom echoes—but morning came, slow and golden. Talking broke the—prayers to God, raw and ragged, tears with my wife, her hand in mine, words to you spilling out like a confession. Her labor, my flush—they're not my shame; they're my story, a bridge for other dads, a lifeline for men who've stood where I stood. You're down, but not out—God's compassion is new every morning, ready to raise you too, to turn your pain into purpose, your silence into strength.

A Father's Redemption

I used to think strength was holding it in—keeping the vault shut, the lid tight. But real strength is letting it out, facing it, naming it. Hannah's not a secret—she's my daughter, a third child I'll see again. My wife's grief was loud, a mother's wail; mine was quiet, a father's whisper—but both were real, both needed air. God didn't just heal her—He healed me, taught me to grieve, to hope, to speak. Job 1:21 says, "The Lord gave and the Lord has taken away; may the name of the Lord be praised." He gave me Hannah, brief as a breath; He took her, but He's giving me back—restored, renewed. Your loss isn't a dead end—it's a detour, a path God's walking with you. Talk about it, man—let it out, let it heal, let it lift you. You're not alone in the down; we're rising together.

Devotional Call to Action: Rising from Man Down

Scripture Reflection: "The Lord is close to the brokenhearted and saves those who are crushed in spirit" (Psalm 34:18, NIV).
Meditation: See yourself down—your loss, your silence, the weight pressing you flat. Feel God close, His hand on your shoulder, steady and warm. Hear Him say, "I save the crushed." Picture rising—not alone, but with Him, with other fathers, their hands outstretched too. Stand in His strength now, tall and sure.
Prayer: Lord, I'm down—man down—from losing my child. I've buried it deep, locked it away, but You see me—every crack, every tear I've held back. Be close, save my crushed spirit. Lift me to grieve, to talk, to heal—give me courage to face it. Help me rise—for my wife, for me, for You. In Jesus' name, Amen.

Action Steps:

1. **Admit**: Tell God one way you're down—one hurt, one fear—trusting Psalm 34:18 to hold you.

2. **Write**: List a suppressed feeling—a moment, a memory—then claim His new mercies over it with Lamentations 3:22-23.

3. **Worship**: Sing "Raise a Hallelujah," loud and bold, shouting over your silence, letting it break.

4. **Connect**: Talk to a man—friend, pastor, brother—about your loss, sharing the load, letting it lift.
Encouragement: Man down doesn't mean out—you're not finished. God's close, saving you, His love unrelenting. Rise—your pain's not wasted; it's purpose, a story to tell. You're healing, father, step by step—up from the down, into His light.

Chapter 12: The Phoenix Who Rises from The Ashes!

A Promise of Restoration

One of the promises of God outlined in Jeremiah 30:17 says, "For I will restore health to you, and I will heal you of your wounds," declares the Lord. This verse emphasizes God's commitment to bring comfort and well-being to those who have suffered. The Hebrew word for "restore" (arukah) means "to recover, to heal, and to restore to health," highlighting God's powerful and comprehensive ability to bring healing and wholeness.

God's Sovereign Comfort

God in His sovereignty consoled us through every part of our loss. His heart till this present day is to ensure every part of our being is made whole. So even though losing Hannah was tumultuous, He did not renege on His Word. You see, it has been six years since our baby went on to be with the Lord. Within that time, I have cried, screamed, laughed, argued, questioned God, and simply come to the realization that it was all in His plans.

Seasons of Solitude

The restoration that has taken place in my life looked different in each season. During the early stages, God had to heal my brokenness. This transpired through personal time with Him, words of encouragement, affirmations, devoted time in prayer, dissecting scriptures on healing, and opening my heart to like-minded believers who assisted in the restoration process.

As time progressed, I had to be honest with the reality that Hannah would never be physically with us again. A hard pill to swallow, but a true story in our lives. Even though the future looked bleak and empty without our precious seed, leaning to Him brought peace to our hearts and hope for the future.

In the next phase, it involved accepting the fact that if we never had another child, purpose would still prevail. Owning up to the fact that when children crossed my path, in my profession as a teacher, I would continue to pour into their lives and guide them into a purpose-filled life! Knowing that if He brought me to it, HE would bring me through it!

Scripture of Meditation

Ecclesiastes 3:1 states, "For everything there is a season, and a time for every activity under heaven." This means that the various circumstances we go through in life are not by incident, but orchestrated or allowed by God with great purpose and intentionality.

Within The Eagle's Eye!

During trials, it's easy to run. But it takes strength to run to the storm and face it, even when you don't know the final outcome. It brings me to the analogy of the eagle.

"Eagles are known for their resilience, and instead of running from storms, they often use the strong winds to rise higher and gain a broader perspective, soaring above the tempest rather than seeking shelter." They [actively] engage with strong winds. This bird is a metaphor to overcome the adversity and the challenges of life! God's hand guided us to be mighty eagles, as He led us higher and higher into His refuge, love, peace, resilience, understanding, and fullness of life, knowing that one day we would be completely restored and able to pour out our heart to others.

Rising Like a Phoenix
In the midst of this trial, I continued in my service as an Intercessor. One of my prayer mates would say, "Every time you pray, I see the Phoenix behind you rising from the ashes!" To rise from the ashes means, "To make a comeback after a disaster that almost led to a tragic end; to make a comeback after a long hiatus; to come back into common use or practice, or back into popularity." Another meaning which touched my heart was "to be renewed after destruction." So what the enemy meant for bad, God turned around for our good.

High Towers of Hope
The healing process with Richard began when the book was being written. He had not dealt with it until that point. For him, it is a day-to-day process, which entails talking about his feelings, unleashing his emotions, seeking God in solace, opening up to the Lord, and sharing his experiences to heal other men in their journey of fatherhood. I can honestly say that it was only the Father that has brought us this far. Without Him, we would not have made it through!

The Heartbeat of Our Story
To share wholeheartedly, without our union of marriage that transpired on Sunday, February 25, 2018, no seed would have been planted. Without the sharp pains that woke me up in the middle of the night, there would have been no exciting pregnancy news. Without the miscarriage, there would be no existent story. But most importantly, without our gracious Hannah, there would be no existent heartbeat—beating vicariously within the pages of this book!

A Renewed Bond
This book reached into the depths of my soul and pulled out emotions I didn't think were still there! It drew my husband and me closer because we had to look each other in the eye and share our thoughts about Hannah. Tears fell, but God prevailed. Frustration flared, but the hand of God was there! Grief was found, but His grace carefully would abound. Hidden feelings were shared, but the Father always cared. So embrace your loss!

Words of Faith
If we could share any words of faith to help you on your journey, it would be: "Go

towards the Father. Allow him to give you wings as eagles! Lean to him, the author and finisher of your faith. Allow him to bring you out of the ashes! Don't Run! Don't Hide! Don't Disappear in Fear! But most importantly, 'Live a Life of Purpose in him!' We did. Because of our surrender, our YES, it is through these divine pages, our spirits, minds and bodies are blessed!"

Devotional Call to Action: Rising as a Phoenix

Scripture Reflection: "For I will restore health to you, and I will heal you of your wounds," declares the Lord (Jeremiah 30:17, NIV); "For everything there is a season, and a time for every activity under heaven" (Ecclesiastes 3:1, NIV).

Meditation: Picture yourself in the ashes of your loss—your pain, your tears, your broken dreams. See God's hand reaching down, lifting you like a phoenix, His winds of grace raising you above the storm. Feel His healing restore your wounds, His purpose renew your spirit. Rise in His strength now, whole and hopeful.

Prayer: Lord, my loss left me in ashes, but You promise restoration. Heal my wounds, renew my health, and lift me from this destruction. Give me wings like an eagle, a heart like a phoenix, to soar above my storm. Restore my purpose, my hope, my joy—make me whole in You. In Jesus' name, Amen.

Action Steps:

- **Reflect:** Sit quietly and write one wound from your loss, then claim Jeremiah 30:17's promise over it, trusting God's healing.

- **Pray:** Whisper, "Lord, lift me from these ashes," and listen for His comfort, picturing yourself rising with eagle's wings.

- **Worship:** Sing "Eagle's Wings" or "Goodness of God," letting His strength renew your spirit as you rise.

- **Share:** Tell a loved one or friend one way God is turning your ashes to beauty, inviting their support in your restoration.
  Encouragement: You're not defeated in the ashes—God's restoring you, raising you like a phoenix. Your loss has a season, but His purpose endures. Rise in Him—He's making you whole, strong, and purposeful again.

Pregnancy Prayer of Protection!

Pregnancy Prayer of Protection: A Healing Walkthrough for Couples

Father, we come before You today as a couple united in love, faith, and purpose.
We thank You for the divine promise of this child growing within the womb, a miracle crafted by Your hands. Lord, Your Word tells us in Psalm 127:3 that children are a heritage from You, a reward from Your heart to ours. We stand in awe of this gift, this sacred life entrusted to us, and we lift our voices in gratitude for Your faithfulness. You have brought this promise to pass in our lives, and we declare with boldness that we will not cast our fruit before its time. The fruits of our ground—our family, our home, our child—will not be destroyed. This will not happen in my life, my spouse's life, nor the life of this precious child we carry together.

We dedicate this child to You, Lord. Your Word in Isaiah 29:11 reminds us, "For I know the plans I have for you, says the Lord, plans to prosper you, plans to give you a hope and a future." We hold fast to this promise as a couple, trusting that the steps of this child are ordered by You. Every heartbeat within me, every movement, every moment of growth is under Your sovereign care. We surrender this little one into Your hands, knowing that Your plans are perfect, Your love is unending, and Your protection is unbreakable.

A Step of Healing: Repentance and Breaking Generational Chains
Father, as we walk this journey together, we pause to seek Your forgiveness and healing. We repent for any sins, transgressions, or evil doings that may have taken root in our lives or the lives of our ancestors. We acknowledge the pain of generational curses—trauma, hurt, molestation, rape, abandonment, or any darkness that may have been passed down through the years. As a couple, we stand united and declare that these chains are broken in the name of Jesus. We will not allow these burdens to fall upon our child. Romans 8:37 assures us that we are more than conquerors through Christ who loves us, and we claim that victory today. Together, we release the past into Your hands, trusting that Your blood cleanses us and sets us free.

Healing Reflection for the Couple:
Take a moment, dear ones, to hold each other's hands. Look into each other's eyes and speak this truth aloud: "We are free in Christ. Our child is free in Christ. No curse has power over us." Let this be a cleansing breath for your marriage—a moment to let go of guilt, shame, or fear. God is rewriting your story with hope.

A Prayer for Health and Strength
Lord, as I carry this seed, I ask You to remember my health. You see every ache, every moment of fatigue, every wave of uncertainty. You know the needs of my body, my mind, and my spirit. I pray for my spouse as well—strengthen them as they stand beside me, supporting and loving me through this season. We lift our other children, if any, into Your care, asking that they too are wrapped in Your peace and protection.

Your Word in Psalm 91:11 promises that You will command Your angels concerning us, to guard us in all our ways. We believe that when we pray, angels move on our behalf, shielding us from harm and bringing Your promises to life.

Declarations of Power and Protection
Father, we declare that every word of power spoken over our lives shall come to pass. Your Word will not fall on stony ground—it will take root and bear fruit in our family. We will not suffer loss. This child will not fall prey to the schemes of the enemy—no murder, no early death, no childhood diseases, no drugs, no molestation, no fatherless home, no homelessness, no neglect, no foster care, no developmental or cognitive disabilities, no cancer, no illness, and no trickery from the adversary will touch them. We speak life over this child, claiming Your promise in Isaiah 54:17: "No weapon formed against them shall prosper."

A Vision for Their Future
Lord, we see this child's future through Your eyes. They will know their purpose and calling at a young age. They will honor their mother and father, fulfilling Your commandment in Exodus 20:12, that their days may be long upon the land. They will walk in the destiny You have placed upon their life—a destiny of joy, impact, and glory for Your name. We pray they grow strong in spirit, wise in heart, and bold in faith, reflecting Your light to the world around them.

A Walkthrough for Healing as a Couple
Pregnancy is a sacred season, but it can also bring challenges—physical strain, emotional shifts, and moments of vulnerability. Let us, as a couple, commit to this healing journey together:

1. **Pause and Listen:** Father, teach us to listen to each other. When words fail, let our hearts hear the unspoken. Help us to be patient, gentle, and kind as we navigate this transformation.
   Healing Step: Sit together in silence for five minutes today. Hold hands, breathe deeply, and let God's peace settle over you.

2. **Speak Life:** Lord, guide our tongues to speak blessings over one another. Let us affirm our love, our strength, and our unity.
   Healing Step: Take turns saying, "I see God's strength in you when…" and finish the sentence with something specific. Let these words build your bond.

3. **Surrender Fear:** God, we give You every worry—about the pregnancy, the delivery, the future. Replace our fear with faith.
   Healing Step: Write down one fear each on a piece of paper. Pray over them together, then tear them up as a symbol of releasing them to God.

4. **Celebrate the Miracle:** Father, remind us to rejoice in this gift. Even on hard days, let gratitude rise in our hearts.

Healing Step: Share one thing you're excited about regarding this child—their laugh, their eyes, their place in your family. Let joy overflow.

A Promise of Light and Healing

Your Word in Isaiah 58:8 declares, "Then your light will break forth like the dawn, and your healing will quickly appear; then your righteousness will go before you, and the glory of the Lord will be your rear guard." We claim this promise, Lord. As we walk this path, let our light—our faith, our love, our hope—shine brightly. Let healing come swiftly to our bodies, our marriage, and our home. Let righteousness lead us, and Your glory protect us from behind.

A Final Declaration Together

Father, we stand as one—husband and wife, mother and father—before Your throne. We declare that this pregnancy is covered by Your blood, this child is sealed by Your Spirit, and our family is surrounded by Your grace. No enemy can stand against Your power in us. We will carry this child to term with joy, deliver them in peace, and raise them in Your truth. Our home is a sanctuary of healing, a testimony of Your goodness, and a legacy of faith for generations to come.
In Jesus' name,
Amen.

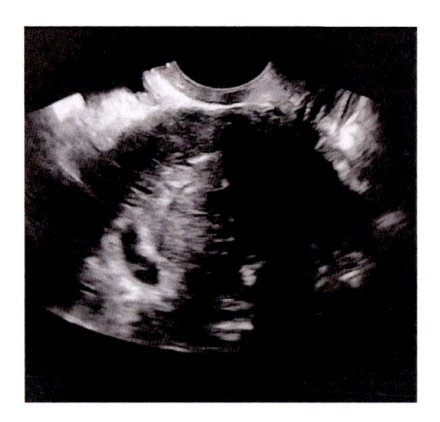

Mommy's
Special Excerpt for Hannah

Hannah, my sweet baby girl, God had other plans for you. Your daddy and I will never forget the day we learned you were growing within me. Our hearts swelled with a joy so full it felt like it might burst. I drank water to nurture you, and you, my little one, craved salads and praline cheesecake—a sweet reminder of the unique bond we shared. I was overjoyed to be your mommy, dreaming of the day I'd raise you alongside your father, a powerhouse duo in the Kingdom of God. Your heartbeat, Hannah, became the pulse of this book—a rhythm that echoes through every page, every prayer, every tear.

A heartbeat is more than a sound. Naturally, it's a symbol of life, a steady cadence proclaiming existence. But biblically, it's so much deeper—it's the core of one's being, the wellspring of true emotions, intentions, and spiritual life. In Scripture, the heart reflects our connection to God, the center from which love, compassion, and devotion flow. Your heartbeat graces the cover of this book, Hannah, not as a marker of loss, but as a tender reminder of the grace God imparted to carry us through. Even though your physical beat stilled, its echo lives on, a testament to the life you held and the purpose you continue to fulfill.

A Treasure of the Heart
The Bible tells us in Luke 6:45, "A good man out of the good treasure of his heart brings forth good, and an evil man out of the evil treasure of his heart brings forth evil; for out of the abundance of the heart his mouth speaks." Hannah, you were a good treasure to us—a gift born of the love that flowed from mommy and daddy's hearts. Though miscarriage stole the chance to hold you in our arms, your heartbeat reverberates across this nation, touching women and men who will cradle this book in their hands. They'll read your story and know that sometimes God's plans shift in ways we can't foresee, but through every loss, He offers healing and restoration. Some will go on to welcome multiple children into their homes, their arms full of laughter and life. For others, that may not be their path. Yet, in every experience, God can bring fullness of joy to hearts open to receive.

Thank You, Hannah Heartbeat
Thank you, my darling, for allowing me to carry you, even for a season. As I write these words in 2025, you would be five years old—a tender age that biblically signifies grace. Your name, Hannah, means "favor" or "grace," a nod to the mother of the prophet Samuel, whose story

reminds us of God's power to turn human weakness into divine strength. This book was destined to be written this year—not just to help mommy and daddy heal, but to reach out to countless others of faith, to address the "elephant in the room" so often ignored: the pain of pregnancy loss. It's a wound too many carry in silence, a grief too often dismissed. But through your life, Hannah, we shine a light on that shadow, offering hope where despair once stood.

To the Parents Who Hold This Book
To every mother and father who turns these pages, know this: the seed you carried mattered. Whether your memory is a baby shower filled with anticipation, a fleeting moment holding your child in your arms, a quiet memorial service, or simply the sound of a heartbeat that once danced in your ears—God had a plan in and through that loss. You are not defined by what you've lost, but by who you are: a warrior, destined to rise above. You were made to take flight, to soar on wings of faith. You are a bridge over troubled waters, guiding others through the storms you've weathered. Above all, you are a parent of divine purpose, strength, and character—a title no one on this earth can strip away.

Keep Believing
Hold fast to this truth: your story isn't over. Whether through the seed of your womb, adoption, in vitro, foster care, or the legacy you leave in others' lives, you can still produce fruit in this earth. Your pain has purpose, your tears have power, and your heart—though scarred—beats with resilience. Hannah taught me that. Her brief life showed me that even in loss, God plants seeds of grace that bloom in unexpected ways.

Hannah Holbert, Our Forever Heartbeat
Hannah, you are forever mommy and daddy's heartbeat. We love you with an ache that time can't erase and a pride that eternity can't dim. Fly high, sweet girl, and reign on high with the King who holds you now. Your life, though short, was a melody of grace, and we'll carry its tune until we see you again.

A Foundation of Hope
In Romans 5:2-5, we find this promise: "Through him we have also obtained access by faith into this grace in which we stand, and we rejoice in hope of the glory of God. Not only that, but we rejoice in our sufferings, knowing that suffering produces endurance, and endurance produces character, and character produces hope, and hope does not put us to shame, because God's love has been poured into our hearts through the Holy Spirit who has been given to us." Let this scripture be your anchor. When loss threatens to overwhelm, stand on this truth. Suffering may come, but it's not the end—it's the beginning of a journey toward endurance, character, and unshakable hope. You are never alone. The Father walks with you, His love poured into your heart by the Spirit who sustains you.

A Closing Prayer
Father, we lift every reader to You—every mother, every father, every heart touched by loss. Wrap them in Your grace, as You did for us through Hannah. Heal the wounds they carry, restore the joy they've lost, and ignite the purpose You've placed within them. Let Hannah's heartbeat echo in their lives, a reminder that You are near, Your plans are good, and Your love never fails. In Jesus' name, Amen.

About the Author

La Tasha Poster-Holbert is a dedicated Dance Teacher and a sought-after Choreographer known throughout various parts of California. In 2010, after receiving several visions through a dream, she launched **Arise Choreography**, a dance company whose slogan is *"We Bring Visions to Life."* Through this company, hundreds of children have been trained in dance technique, leadership skills, biblical principles, split technique, choreography essentials, and core life concepts to help them succeed.

She has served as an educator in multiple school districts across Los Angeles, California, for the past 17 years, teaching a wide range of dance genres including Ballet, Modern, Lyrical, Tap, Jazz, African, Gymnastics, Praise Dance, Choreographic Principles, and Stretch Technique. Her teaching experience also extends internationally—having taught dance in the Republic of South Korea at Osan and Kunsan Air Force Bases to adults from around the world.

Mrs. Poster-Holbert currently serves as a **Child Development Teacher at Culver City High School**. She holds degrees in Theatre Arts and Dance (with a concentration in dance), as well as an Associate of Arts degree in Business Management. In 2021, she earned Career Technical Education Credentials in the areas of **Arts, Media & Entertainment**, **Child Development & Family Services**, and **Business & Marketing**.

In 2022, she was honored to be one of the featured authors in *Let the Women Speak, Volume II*, where her chapter focused on overcoming loss and triumphing through Christ.

La Tasha received her ministerial license in **December 2020** and again in **2024**, equipping her to impart biblical principles and guide others in their walk with God. For the past five years, she has faithfully served in various ministerial roles including Prayer, Deliverance, Gospel Teaching, Praise Dance, and Scribing.

A passionate creative, La Tasha expresses herself through vivid imagery and movement, with a heartfelt mission to bring healing to the world through **arts, design, and dance**.

This is her story!

A Heartfelt Thank You from LaTasha and Richard

Dear Reader,

From the depths of our hearts, thank you for purchasing *Hannah's Heartbeat*. This book is more than pages and words—it's our tears, our prayers, our shattered dreams, and the grace that pieced us back together. When you chose to hold this story in your hands, you didn't just buy a book; you welcomed our little Hannah into your life, her heartbeat echoing through every chapter, every line, every breath we've poured onto these pages.

Many years ago, we stood in a place of unimaginable loss, a silent bathroom where our world broke apart. LaTasha carried Hannah in her womb; I, Richard, carried the weight of her absence in my silence. We wept alone, together, and in ways we couldn't even name. But God—our refuge, our healer—met us there. He took our ashes and gave us beauty, our mourning and gave us joy. This book is that beauty, that joy, born from the pain we thought would consume us.

To you, who may carry your own silent grief, or stand beside someone who does, thank you for letting us share this with you. Every tear we've shed, every prayer we've whispered, every moment we've risen from the ashes—it's all here, not just for us, but for you. You've given us the privilege of speaking Hannah's name aloud, of letting her purpose touch your heart, and for that, we are forever grateful. She was our gift, brief but eternal, and now, through your hands, her heartbeat lives on.

We pray that as you turn these pages, you feel God's nearness as we did—His promise to restore, to heal, to lift you like an eagle above the storm. Thank you for walking this journey with us, for holding our story close, for giving us a chance to rise together. From the bottom of our souls, with all the love and grace Hannah brought us, thank you.

With heartfelt gratitude,
LaTasha and Richard Holbert

Your Healing Journey Begins Here!

A Journey Through Grief: A Reflective Course Based on *Hannah's Heartbeat*

Welcome to this reflective course inspired by *Hannah's Heartbeat*. Miscarriage can leave a hidden wound, often borne in silence. This course helps you determine if you're silently dealing with grief through 50 yes-or-no questions about your experience. Answer each with a simple "yes" (1 point) or "no" (0 points), tallying your score as you go. A "yes" suggests a sign of silent grief—suppression, triggers, or isolation. At the end, an analysis key interprets your score and offers resources if you need support. Answer honestly; this is your tool to uncover and heal.

Section 1: The Initial Impact (Questions 1-10)

1. Did you feel overwhelmed or numb when you learned your pregnancy ended?
2. Did you think "This can't be happening" when you saw or heard there was no heartbeat?
3. Did your body feel heavy or unwell in the hours or days after your miscarriage?
4. Were you angry or sad leaving the doctor's office or hospital?
5. Did you feel awkward or detached when you first told someone about your loss?
6. Did seeing your reflection or empty womb make you feel empty or strange?
7. Did people's silence about your loss frustrate or hurt you?
8. Did returning home after losing your baby feel lonely or wrong?
9. Did your hopes for parenthood feel crushed in that moment?
10. Do you vividly remember physical pain or discomfort from that time?

Section 2: The Weight of Silence (Questions 11-20)

11. Do you feel upset when others avoid mentioning your miscarriage?
12. Do comments like "You can try again" annoy or sadden you?
13. Does seeing pregnant women or young children make you feel resentful or sad?
14. Do you feel heavy or anxious when alone with thoughts of your loss?
15. Do you feel ignored when people act like nothing happened?
16. Does keeping your pain private feel isolating or burdensome?
17. Has silence about your miscarriage strained your relationships?
18. Do baby items or reminders trigger sadness or avoidance in you?
19. Does hearing "miscarriage" in conversation stir discomfort or pain?
20. Do you feel a pang in your heart when you avoid talking about your baby?

Section 3: The Burden of Strength (Questions 21-30)

21. Did you feel pressured to "be strong" for someone else after your loss?
22. Was it hard to hold back tears or emotions to avoid seeming weak?
23. Do you feel irritated when expected to move on quickly?
24. Do you feel guilty focusing on your partner's needs over your own?
25. Does hiding your pain because it's "expected" exhaust you?
26. Do you feel drained pushing grief aside for daily tasks?

27. Did you feel trapped when you couldn't express your sadness openly?
28. Was pretending everything was fine after your loss stressful?
29. Do you feel judged when pressured to "man up" or "get over it"?
30. Does suppressing your hurt to protect others weigh on you?

Section 4: The Lingering Shadows (Questions 31-40)

31. Do days like Mother's Day, Father's Day, or your due date hurt you?
32. Do you feel sad imagining what your child might have been like?
33. Does seeing an empty nursery space make you ache?
34. Do holidays or milestones feel empty without your baby?
35. Do unexpected memories of your loss overwhelm you?
36. Did facing the place of your miscarriage upset you?
37. Do you feel hopeless thinking of a future without your child?
38. Do memories of the physical loss (e.g., labor, passing) still haunt you?
39. Do dreams of your baby or waking expecting them stir pain?
40. Do you avoid places or things tied to your pregnancy because they hurt?

Section 5: The Path to Healing (Questions 41-50)

41. Do you feel hesitant to talk about your miscarriage, even with someone safe?
42. Was letting yourself cry or scream about your loss difficult?
43. Do you avoid asking "Why did this happen?" out of fear or doubt?
44. Does thinking your baby had a purpose feel distant or hard to accept?
45. Do you struggle to imagine rising above your pain?
46. Does leaning into faith or hope for healing feel uncertain?
47. Are you reluctant to share your story with another grieving parent?
48. Has finding peace after your loss been rare or fleeting?
49. Do you resist embracing your grief instead of fighting it?
50. Does being whole again feel impossible or far away?

Analysis Key: Are You Silently Dealing with Grief?

Tally Your Score: Count 1 point for each "yes" answer (0 for "no"). Total your points out of 50, then use this guide to assess if you're silently grieving and need help.

Scoring System (0-50 Points):

- **0-10 Points (Low Silent Grief)**: Few signs of silent grief—you may be processing openly or healing well. Any "yes" answers are areas to watch.
- **11-25 Points (Moderate Silent Grief)**: Some grief is silent, with triggers or suppression present. You're managing but could benefit from support.
- **26-50 Points (High Silent Grief)**: Strong signs of silent grief—you're carrying a heavy, unvoiced burden. Seek help now; your pain needs attention.

Signs of Silent Grief (1 Point per "Yes"):

1. **Suppression**: "Yes" to hiding emotions (e.g., Q21, Q27) = holding back to "be strong."
2. **Persistent Triggers**: "Yes" to ongoing pain from reminders (e.g., Q31, Q35) = unprocessed grief lingering.
3. **Isolation**: "Yes" to feeling alone or ignored (e.g., Q11, Q16) = silence isolating you.
4. **Unspoken Loss**: "Yes" to deep, unshared feelings (e.g., Q32, Q38) = grief locked inside.
5. **Resistance to Healing**: "Yes" to avoiding healing steps (e.g., Q41, Q49) = reluctance to move forward.

What Your Score Means:

- **0-10**: You're likely open or healing. Reflect on "yes" answers—small steps (e.g., journaling) can help.
- **11-25**: You're holding some grief back. Try opening up (e.g., talk to a friend) to ease it.
- **26+**: You're silently struggling—reach out for help now (see resources below). You're not alone.

Resources for Help (Online as of March 31, 2025):

- **Postpartum Support International (PSI)**: Free helpline (1-800-944-4773, text 800-944-4773) and online groups for pregnancy loss. postpartum.net.
- **Miscarriage Association**: Helpline (01924 200799) and forums for miscarriage support. miscarriageassociation.org.uk.
- **Share Pregnancy & Infant Loss Support**: Local and online communities for grieving parents. nationalshare.org.
- **The Compassionate Friends**: Support groups for child loss. compassionatefriends.org.
- **Pregnancy Loss Support Program (NCJW NY)**: Free counseling and groups. pregnancyloss.org, 212-687-5030.

Next Steps:

- **26+**: Call a helpline (e.g., PSI) or join a group today—start healing with support.
- **11-25**: Explore a resource (e.g., Share's forums) or talk to someone this week.
- **0-10**: Keep progressing—use resources if a "yes" resurfaces.

Your grief is valid. This score is your guide—help is here when you need it.

You're not alone. Your grief matters, and help is here when you're ready.

-La Tasha

31 Days of Prayer for Healing

31 Days of Prayer for Healing from Loss: A Journal Inspired by *Hannah's Heartbeat*

Welcome to this 31-day prayer journal, crafted to guide you through healing after miscarriage. Loss can leave a quiet wound, but God's Word offers solace, strength, and renewal. Each day, you'll find a scripture to read, a brief reflection to ponder, and a prayer to speak—tools to help you rise from the ashes of grief. Use this journal daily: read the scripture aloud, reflect in silence or write your thoughts, and pray with an open heart. Let these moments draw you closer to healing, purpose, and peace.

Day 1: God's Nearness

- **Scripture**: Psalm 34:18 - "The Lord is close to the brokenhearted and saves those who are crushed in spirit."
- **Reflection**: Your heart may feel shattered, but God is nearer than your breath, ready to hold you in your pain.
- **Prayer**: Lord, my heart is broken from this loss. Be close to me today—save my crushed spirit with Your gentle presence. Amen.

Day 2: Restored Health

- **Scripture**: Jeremiah 30:17 - "For I will restore health to you, and I will heal you of your wounds," declares the Lord.
- **Reflection**: God promises to mend what's torn—your body, your spirit, your hope—step by step.
- **Prayer**: Father, my wounds feel deep. Restore my health, heal me inside and out, as only You can. Amen.

Day 3: A Time for Healing

- **Scripture**: Ecclesiastes 3:1-4 - "For everything there is a season… a time to weep, and a time to laugh; a time to mourn, and a time to dance."
- **Reflection**: This season of weeping is real, but healing has its time too—trust God's timing.
- **Prayer**: God, this is my time to mourn. Guide me through this season to a time of healing and joy. Amen.

Day 4: Strength in Weakness

- **Scripture**: 2 Corinthians 12:9 - "My grace is sufficient for you, for my power is made perfect in weakness."

- **Reflection**: Your weakness isn't failure—it's where God's strength shines brightest.
- **Prayer**: Lord, I feel weak from this loss. Let Your grace be enough—make Your power perfect in me today. Amen.

Day 5: Peace Beyond Understanding

- **Scripture**: Philippians 4:7 - "And the peace of God, which transcends all understanding, will guard your hearts and your minds in Christ Jesus."
- **Reflection**: Peace can feel distant, but God offers it freely, guarding your heart even now.
- **Prayer**: Jesus, my mind races and my heart aches. Guard me with Your peace that I can't comprehend. Amen.

Day 6: Casting Your Cares

- **Scripture**: 1 Peter 5:7 - "Cast all your anxiety on him because he cares for you."
- **Reflection**: Your worries don't have to stay buried—God invites you to release them to Him.
- **Prayer**: Father, I'm anxious and hurting. I cast this pain on You—carry it for me, for You care. Amen.

Day 7: A Refuge in Trouble

- **Scripture**: Psalm 46:1 - "God is our refuge and strength, an ever-present help in trouble."
- **Reflection**: In the storm of loss, God is your safe place, your strength when you're down.
- **Prayer**: God, this trouble overwhelms me. Be my refuge, my strength—help me now. Amen.

Day 8: Joy After Weeping

- **Scripture**: Psalm 30:5 - "Weeping may stay for the night, but rejoicing comes in the morning."
- **Reflection**: The night of grief is long, but joy's dawn is promised—hold on.
- **Prayer**: Lord, my weeping lingers. Bring the morning of joy to my heart soon. Amen.

Day 9: Beauty for Ashes

- **Scripture**: Isaiah 61:3 - "To provide for those who grieve… a crown of beauty instead of ashes."
- **Reflection**: Your ashes of loss can become something beautiful—God's transforming you.
- **Prayer**: Father, my grief feels like ashes. Give me beauty instead—crown me with Your hope. Amen.

Day 10: Hope and a Future

- **Scripture**: Jeremiah 29:11 - "For I know the plans I have for you… plans to give you hope and a future."
- **Reflection**: Loss isn't the end—God has plans to restore your hope.
- **Prayer**: God, I feel hopeless. Show me Your plans—give me a future I can trust. Amen.

Day 11: Binding the Broken

- **Scripture**: Psalm 147:3 - "He heals the brokenhearted and binds up their wounds."
- **Reflection**: Every crack in your heart is seen—God's binding them with care.
- **Prayer**: Lord, my heart's broken, my wounds raw. Heal me, bind me up with Your love. Amen.

Day 12: Everlasting Love

- **Scripture**: Jeremiah 31:3 - "I have loved you with an everlasting love; I have drawn you with unfailing kindness."
- **Reflection**: You're held by a love that never fades, even in loss.
- **Prayer**: God, I need Your love. Draw me close with Your kindness—hold me forever. Amen.

Day 13: Rest for the Weary

- **Scripture**: Matthew 11:28 - "Come to me, all you who are weary and burdened, and I will give you rest."
- **Reflection**: Your burden is heavy—Jesus offers rest if you come.
- **Prayer**: Jesus, I'm weary from this loss. I come to You—give me rest today. Amen.

Day 14: A Child's Purpose

- **Scripture**: Matthew 19:14 - "Let the little children come to me… for the kingdom of heaven belongs to such as these."
- **Reflection**: Your baby's brief life has purpose in God's kingdom—trust His care.
- **Prayer**: Lord, my child is with You. Let their purpose comfort me—hold them close. Amen.

Day 15: New Mercies

- **Scripture**: Lamentations 3:22-23 - "Because of the Lord's great love we are not consumed, for his compassions never fail. They are new every morning."
- **Reflection**: Each day brings fresh mercy—your loss won't consume you.
- **Prayer**: Father, I feel consumed. Pour Your new mercies on me this morning. Amen.

Day 16: Strengthened by Faith

- **Scripture**: Isaiah 40:31 - "Those who hope in the Lord will renew their strength. They will soar on wings like eagles."
- **Reflection**: Hope can lift you higher than this pain—God's renewing you.
- **Prayer**: God, my strength is gone. Renew me—lift me on eagle's wings with hope. Amen.

Day 17: Comfort in Sorrow

- **Scripture**: 2 Corinthians 1:3-4 - "The God of all comfort, who comforts us in all our troubles, so that we can comfort others."
- **Reflection**: Your sorrow has a purpose—to receive and share comfort.
- **Prayer**: Lord, comfort me in this trouble. Use it so I can comfort others too. Amen.

Day 18: Eternal Reunion

- **Scripture**: Revelation 21:4 - "He will wipe every tear from their eyes. There will be no more death or mourning."
- **Reflection**: One day, tears end—your loss isn't forever; reunion awaits.
- **Prayer**: God, my tears are many. Wipe them one day—hold my baby until I'm there. Amen.

Day 19: Trust Amid Loss

- **Scripture**: Job 1:21 - "The Lord gave and the Lord has taken away; may the name of the Lord be praised."
- **Reflection**: Loss tests trust—praising God can anchor you through it.
- **Prayer**: Lord, You gave and took away. Help me trust and praise You still. Amen.

Day 20: A Steadfast Anchor

- **Scripture**: Hebrews 6:19 - "We have this hope as an anchor for the soul, firm and secure."
- **Reflection**: Hope steadies your soul when grief shakes it—cling to it.
- **Prayer**: Jesus, my soul's adrift. Be my anchor—keep me firm and secure. Amen.

Day 21: God's Faithfulness

- **Scripture**: Deuteronomy 7:9 - "Know therefore that the Lord your God is God; he is the faithful God."
- **Reflection**: God's faithfulness doesn't waver, even in your loss—He's with you.
- **Prayer**: Faithful God, I feel lost. Show me Your steady love today. Amen.

Day 22: Light in Darkness

- **Scripture**: Psalm 18:28 - "You, Lord, keep my lamp burning; my God turns my darkness into light."
- **Reflection**: Darkness feels thick, but God lights your way—look for it.
- **Prayer**: Lord, this darkness blinds me. Keep my lamp burning—turn it to light. Amen.

Day 23: Peaceful Sleep

- **Scripture**: Psalm 4:8 - "In peace I will lie down and sleep, for you alone, Lord, make me dwell in safety."
- **Reflection**: Rest can heal—God guards your sleep with peace.
- **Prayer**: God, my nights are restless. Grant me peace to sleep safely in You. Amen.

Day 24: Strengthened Heart

- **Scripture**: Psalm 73:26 - "My flesh and my heart may fail, but God is the strength of my heart."
- **Reflection**: Your heart may falter, but God's strength sustains it.

- **Prayer**: Lord, my heart fails me. Be its strength—hold me up today. Amen.

Day 25: Unfailing Love

- **Scripture**: Psalm 36:7 - "How priceless is your unfailing love, O God!"
- **Reflection**: God's love never fails you, even when grief clouds your view.
- **Prayer**: God, I need Your love. Let its priceless worth wrap me now. Amen.

Day 26: A Living Hope

- **Scripture**: 1 Peter 1:3 - "He has given us new birth into a living hope."
- **Reflection**: Loss births pain, but God births hope—alive and growing.
- **Prayer**: Jesus, my hope died with my loss. Give me new, living hope today. Amen.

Day 27: God's Presence

- **Scripture**: Psalm 16:11 - "In your presence there is fullness of joy."
- **Reflection**: Joy hides in God's presence—seek it there, even now.
- **Prayer**: Lord, I crave joy. Draw me into Your presence—fill me there. Amen.

Day 28: Renewed Spirit

- **Scripture**: Psalm 51:10 - "Create in me a pure heart, O God, and renew a steadfast spirit within me."
- **Reflection**: Your spirit can be renewed—God's remaking you from within.
- **Prayer**: God, my spirit's weary. Create a pure heart, renew me steadfastly. Amen.

Day 29: Everlasting Arms

- **Scripture**: Deuteronomy 33:27 - "The eternal God is your refuge, and underneath are the everlasting arms."
- **Reflection**: You're held by arms that never tire—rest in them.
- **Prayer**: Eternal God, I'm falling. Catch me in Your everlasting arms today. Amen.

Day 30: A Song of Deliverance

- **Scripture**: Psalm 32:7 - "You are my hiding place; you will protect me from trouble and surround me with songs of deliverance."
- **Reflection**: God hides you in His care, singing over your pain—listen.

- **Prayer**: Lord, hide me from this trouble. Surround me with Your song of deliverance. Amen.

Day 31: Complete Restoration

- **Scripture**: Joel 2:25 - "I will repay you for the years the locusts have eaten."
- **Reflection**: God restores what loss stole—your healing is His promise kept.
- **Prayer**: God, my years feel eaten by loss. Repay me with restoration—make me whole.

Amen!

A Heartfelt Thank You from LaTasha and Richard

Dear Reader,

From the depths of our hearts, thank you for purchasing *Hannah's Heartbeat*. This book is more than pages and words—it's our tears, our prayers, our shattered dreams, and the grace that pieced us back together. When you chose to hold this story in your hands, you didn't just buy a book; you welcomed our little Hannah into your life, her heartbeat echoing through every chapter, every line, every breath we've poured onto these pages.

Many years ago, we stood in a place of unimaginable loss, a silent bathroom where our world broke apart. LaTasha carried Hannah in her womb; I, Richard, carried the weight of her absence in my silence. We wept alone, together, and in ways we couldn't even name. But God—our refuge, our healer—met us there. He took our ashes and gave us beauty, our mourning and gave us joy. This book is that beauty, that joy, born from the pain we thought would consume us.

To you, who may carry your own silent grief, or stand beside someone who does, thank you for letting us share this with you. Every tear we've shed, every prayer we've whispered, every moment we've risen from the ashes—it's all here, not just for us, but for you. You've given us the privilege of speaking Hannah's name aloud, of letting her purpose touch your heart, and for that, we are forever grateful. She was our gift, brief but eternal, and now, through your hands, her heartbeat lives on.

We pray that as you turn these pages, you feel God's nearness as we did—His promise to restore, to heal, to lift you like an eagle above the storm. Thank you for walking this journey with us, for holding our story close, for giving us a chance to rise together. From the bottom of our souls, with all the love and grace Hannah brought us, thank you.

With heartfelt gratitude,
LaTasha and Richard Holbert

Made in the USA
Monee, IL
27 April 2025

aba426d9-ffc7-4edc-aa25-9172b6b35ebeR01